GUN to the HEAD

T0386562

GUN *to the* HEAD

MY LIFE AS A TACTICAL COP.
THE IMPACT. THE AFTERMATH.

KEITH BANKS

ALLEN&UNWIN
SYDNEY · MELBOURNE · AUCKLAND · LONDON

Certain names and details have been changed to protect the guilty and innocent alike.

Allen & Unwin
83 Alexander Street
Crows Nest NSW 2065
Australia
Phone: (61 2) 8425 0100
Email: info@allenandunwin.com
Web: www.allenandunwin.com

A catalogue record for this book is available from the National Library of Australia

ISBN 978 1 76106 512 5

Set in 12/16.7pt Minion by Midland Typesetters, Australia
Printed and bound in Australia by McPherson's Printing Group

10 9 8 7 6 5 4 3 2 1

Dedicated to all police officers, current, veteran and future.
You do things others cannot. Thank you for your service.

Whoever fights monsters should see to it that in the process he does not become a monster. And if you gaze long enough into an abyss, the abyss will gaze back into you.

Friedrich Nietzsche

It's usually a Glock but sometimes it's my old Smith and Wesson .38. The scenes change but have one constant: I am in immediate danger and the weight of the weapon in my hand is comforting and familiar. I aim at my enemy and squeeze the trigger, but it is locked in place. I continue to squeeze the trigger, willing it to move, but it remains frozen. The gun is useless and I'm defenceless.

I wake in fright, my pulse pounding, my eyes wide. I take deep breaths to calm myself and it takes a few seconds to register that I'm in my bed, safe and secure. My mind drifts back to all those years ago and there's no more sleep for me.

The dreams are fewer these days but come unbidden, just like the waves of sadness that ebb and flow without cause or remedy.

Such is the dark legacy of PTSD.

PROLOGUE

27 July 1987

I arrived at the Tactical Response Group (TRG) office in Alderley on Monday morning for my normal 8 am to 4 pm shift. The moment I got there, Inspector Harry Edwards asked to see me in his office. I walked upstairs and was told to close the door behind me. Sergeant John Watt, a part-time member of the TRG, was sitting in a chair near the boss's desk.

I greeted John. He looked sombre and nodded hello.

Harry was direct. 'We've got a job on and if it goes ahead, it's probably going to be the most serious one we've done.'

The month before I'd been sent to the Special Air Service Regiment in Perth to attend the Police Assault Group Counter Terrorist Instructor's Course. I'd spent two weeks learning how to teach tactics and plan operations, and also practiced live fire close-quarter battle in the killing house. Selected operators from each state were on the course, and we learned how to smash our way into strongholds using stun grenades, tear gas and submachine guns, moving quickly in the darkness, identifying hostile targets and engaging them.

I was twenty-nine years old and on top of my game. I'd been a successful undercover cop and was now full-time in tactical response. I had total faith in my own abilities. That sounds arrogant, but I was working at the sharp end of policing and treated it accordingly. Hearing the boss say it was going to be serious gave me that familiar rush, knowing there'd be danger, adrenaline and fear, but I was also a professional. This was what my job was.

'Okay boss, what have we got?'

Harry had briefed John already. I soon realised why John wasn't saying much.

'This stays in this room for the time being,' Harry said. 'The CIB has a possible address on Paul James Mullin, a violent armed robber who's good for at least two stickups on banks here. He's an escapee from Long Bay and he's been on the run since 1978. He's a violent bastard and interstate detectives say he will not hesitate to shoot.' Harry handed me a thick manila folder containing Mullin's criminal history.

My pulse quickened as I read the pages. Mullin had robbed his first bank in 1972. He was arrested soon after and sentenced to ten years. He was released on parole after three. In 1977 he started robbing banks again, becoming increasingly violent with each robbery. Then, in late 1977, he shot and crippled a security guard standing outside a Sydney bank with no provocation or warning. He'd been arrested and placed on remand in Long Bay gaol while awaiting trial.

Not long afterwards, Mullin and another inmate staged a violent escape, bashing a building contractor and stealing his vehicle. Since then, Mullin had been moving between Queensland, New South Wales and Western Australia using several stolen identities and funding his lifestyle with armed robberies. He was a skilled bushman and spent long periods living in the scrub, always managing to keep one step ahead of the police. His abandoned campsites were often found with weapons stashed nearby.

On 2 July 1987, Mullin robbed a Suncorp bank in Toombul Shopping Town. As he was making his getaway, he was tackled by a brave passer-by. They wrestled for control of a sawn-off Ruger Mini-14 .223 calibre rifle, but Mullin got the upper hand and fled. He took the rifle with him, leaving almost thirty thousand dollars in a bag on the footpath.

That night, in a display of astounding naivety, the passer-by was interviewed on television. His full name and the suburb he lived in were broadcast.

Harry explained that Mullin was living at 38 Walter Street, Virginia with his de facto partner, Susan Theresa Clarke, and her two sons. Clarke was his accomplice and driver in the armed robberies. The information had come from a 67-year-old woman employed as a part-time nanny who had been in the house when Mullin saw the interview. 'You don't know who I am, but I know who you are,' he had yelled. 'I'm going to square up with this bastard and fucking kill him.'

Clarke had told the woman about Mullin's real identity, and she'd seen guns in the house. His outburst scared her so much that she'd felt compelled to act. She went straight to the Redcliffe police and asked to speak to detectives.

'If it is Mullin,' Harry said, 'we need to plan how we take him out. The code name for this operation is Flashdance.'

John and I looked at each other. I already had the feeling that this wasn't like other raids, and I could tell from John's expression that he felt the same. 'Okay,' I said. 'Let's start on the Operation Order.'

'You need to think about who you want to go in,' John said, looking at me intently. 'Make sure they're the right blokes.' I knew what he meant. I needed to pick the best of the group, men who were focused and switched on who wouldn't take a backward step. The TRG had executed hundreds of forced entries and responded to numerous sieges but had never fired a shot in anger. 'There's a fucking good chance this is going to go hot, Banksy.'

My journey to this point had been a path not trodden by many cops. I'd always wanted to work in areas that were full of action and excitement. That urge had taken me at the age of twenty-one into deep undercover, where I'd been changed forever. After I returned to the world of normal policing, I'd needed to find that addictive rush of adrenaline again. The next logical step for me was to seek out the world of special weapons and tactical operations.

Fear and exhilaration are blood brothers; that's what drives risk.

I should have been careful what I'd wished for.

TARINGA, 1984

The Taringa Criminal Investigation Branch (CIB) might have begun as my exile from the Drug Squad but it became my salvation instead.

From the day I started at the Police Academy as a sixteen-year-old cadet in 1975, I'd wanted to be a super cop and to work in the Drug Squad to fight the drug trade, which I saw as an immense evil. After I'd been on the road in uniform for almost three years, I volunteered and was accepted for deep undercover work in the Drug Squad. Little did I know on my first day how it would ultimately change me. I transformed from a non-drinking, idealistic young recruit to a binge drinking, pot smoking undercover cop. I masqueraded as a heroin dealer, a gunman, a bikie associate or whatever cover each operation demanded. I lost the innocence I had once possessed but in return I gained a more realistic understanding of the world, as challenging as that reality was. It was no longer simply black and white but became shades of grey; not all crooks were bad and not all cops were good. The only police I could trust were my circle of other undercover cops; each of us had experienced the corruption of certain detectives and senior police and we knew we could only really rely on each other.

My opinion of drugs also changed. No longer did I consider everyone who smoked dope to be a drug fiend, but I also saw first hand the scourge of heroin on many lives. My undercover friend Harry had been forced to use heroin as part of his cover and had become an addict. He later left the Job and embarked on armed robberies to support his habit. A habit directly caused by his time as an undercover cop. Harry was lost. It would be years before any of us would see him again.

When I'd had enough of undercover, I returned to uniform for a few months, gradually adapting to a version of normal life again. I applied to the CIB and worked my way back to the Drug Squad, this time as a detective. I ran undercover operations, making sure I looked after the welfare of undercover operatives as best I could, something that was not a priority when I was undercover. I'm certain Harry had been supplied with heroin by police because it suited them to have an undercover who could be put in situations where heroin use was necessary. Other undercovers who were clearly burnt out were moved from job to job without regard to their welfare. On one of my first undercover buys I'd been forced to use speed at gunpoint, and when I reported it the next day I was not asked if I was okay. The only thing the detective handling the job was interested in was that the target had a gun. Undercovers were treated like collateral damage and I wanted to do as much as I could to change that. (Later I would become one of the first instructors on a Covert Police Operatives training course, but that was still a long time in the future.)

I was on my guard with some members of the Drug Squad. While I was undercover, I had refused an approach from some officers to sell seized heroin and split the profits and I knew they'd be watching me, concerned I'd give them up. But in those days of not knowing who was honest, my best method of surviving was to keep my mouth shut.

Larry McGregor, one of my closest friends, was still working undercover and was fast burning out. He and I had been in Cairns to infiltrate the drug scene and, although I was designated as Larry's controller and exhibit officer, I started working side by side with him. I had jumped at the chance to experience the rush and fear of living a fake life one last time. We discovered the target we were setting up to buy over $100,000 worth of drugs was a prison escapee who was planning to murder both of us for the money. He had some experience in that area; he had been sentenced to life for a double murder. The paradox was that the three of us actually had a good time together, apart from the whole planned homicide thing.

Following that operation I ran a job on the Gold Coast utilising an informant. Harry was the undercover. (I would later learn that this was when he was deep in his well-hidden addiction.) When the informant started boasting to his mates that he was working with an undercover cop, I quickly shut him down and removed him from the job. The operation concluded successfully a couple of months later with a buy bust. I assumed all was well, until a detective sergeant in the office demanded I authorise the payment of a cash reward to the informant, who had put Harry's life in danger. I refused, but I wasn't prepared for the penalty of going against the tide. I was shown the door.

The cynic in me might have thought that perhaps that money was to be shared between the informant and his handler. In 1980s Queensland anything was possible. It wouldn't have been the first time the tentacles of corruption had slithered along the corridors of the Drug Squad.

My transfer to the Taringa CIB was punishment for failing to toe the line, whatever the line was. To say I was pissed off is an understatement. I was angry, disappointed and resentful that honesty, integrity and my concern for my undercover agent didn't get me anywhere. It seemed that all my previous work and personal sacrifice counted for nought.

My first few weeks at Taringa were spent in a fug of bitter self-pity. Stupid really, because whoever had me transferred had unwittingly done me a huge favour. This was where I learned to be a real detective and had a ton of fun along the way. In that suburban CIB office, I finally worked with a crew I could trust.

Like many other police stations in 1990s Queensland, the Taringa CIB office was an old, converted house. It was a typical Queenslander, raised high on stumps to take advantage of the breezes, with a weatherboard exterior, casement windows and gable-style tin roof. A big gate on the left opened to allow cars access to parking in the large yard at the rear of the house. Half a dozen stairs led to the front door, which was left open during the day to reveal the reception desk behind which sat a public servant who dealt with inquiries. A room had been added underneath for the storage of exhibits and the remaining area was perfect for drinks. A large second-hand beer fridge had been installed beside the exhibit room and was evidently well used.

Taringa was run by Detective Sergeant First Class Bob Dallow. Bob was a solidly built man in his forties with a bald head, a beaming smile and a very interesting way of keeping his detectives on their toes. I experienced this on day one. I arrived at the office shortly before 8.00 am and Bob called me into his office, which was located behind the reception desk, to confirm I was there on permanent transfer even though I'd been told by the Drug Squad boss it was only for six weeks. I couldn't hide my disappointment.

My paranoia kicked in. Had I been transferred because I refused to sell heroin for corrupt cops? Was it because I refused to sign off on reward money for an informant and his police handler wanted a cut of the cash? I was jolted by the realisation that I couldn't save the world. I felt weary. Fuck it. I tried to put on a positive face.

I looked at Bob and quietly said, 'Sorry, boss. My mistake.'

He looked back at me steadily. 'You're better off with us, mate. Believe me.'

With that, he glanced over my shoulder and said, 'Sorry madam, I'll be with you in a moment.' I turned to look at the reception counter and felt a resounding smack to the back of my head. The force pushed me forward and I turned back to Bob, my hands instinctively in a fighting position. He was grinning from ear to ear, 'Don't trust anyone. My detectives don't get sucked in. And now you're one of my detectives.' Even today it makes me smile; that was Bob's manner of endearment and hearing him tell me I was one of the crew made me feel wanted, even though my head felt like it had been hit with a telephone book.

I was introduced to the rest of the office team. They were all strangers to me but immediately made me welcome. Bob partnered me with Peter, a detective sergeant who was an old school copper in his mid-forties with grey hair and relaxed attitude.

He shook my hand. 'G'day, mate, welcome to Taringa, let's have a cuppa.'

Over a cup of tea Peter gave me an overview of the office. 'This is the most active CIB office in Brisbane. You don't last long here if you're a dud. Bob told me about the Druggies and the work you did. It looks to me like you've been shafted but I don't give a fuck about them. You're my offsider and that's all that matters. This is a good crew of blokes and we look after each other.' Still on my guard, I nodded at the appropriate times. I'd been hyper vigilant since starting as an undercover operative and nothing had changed. I hoped what Peter said was true.

'By the way, don't fall for Bob's look behind you trick. He hits like a fucking wrecking ball'. I grinned at him, 'Too late, mate.' My head was still ringing.

Our CIB division covered the leafy middle-class suburbs of Taringa, Toowong, Indooroopilly, St Lucia, Chapel Hill, Kenmore, Brookfield and Mt Coot-tha. These suburbs were some of the wealthiest in Brisbane, making them a honey pot for break and enter offenders. Taringa's area also included the Royal Exchange Hotel, where I had spent many long hours as an undercover operative buying heroin, weed, acid, hash and any other illicit drug I could get. I made a mental note to pay this pub my personal attention when I could. I was looking forward to walking into the beer garden as a detective and not as a fake drug dealer.

True to Peter's word, the office was constantly busy and dealt with everything from minor thefts to more serious crime including rape and robbery. Peter was a calming influence on me, which is what I desperately needed. I'd been addicted to the fear and excitement of undercover and was still looking for ways to get that hit, but he taught me to take my time with an investigation. Police work wasn't only about kicking in doors and grabbing bad guys, it was about methodical and often boring work to make sure offenders didn't have any chance of squirming their way out of charges in court.

Denis Horne had been a military police serviceman in Vietnam. He was in his late thirties, solidly built and around 175 centimetres, with the regulation moustache favoured by many cops. Denis was partnered with Dan, who was also in his late thirties. Dan was much taller, lean and strong. He was quiet and laconic and would have been at home in the Queensland bush droving cattle. Each complemented the other. They were rarely idle and had a network of informants throughout the division. A typical day would see Denis stroll into the office I shared with Peter holding a search warrant. 'Okay, men, we've got another one. You coming?' he'd say with a familiar twinkle in his eye.

It only took a few weeks for me to stop feeling like an outsider. Each day was different, and I started looking forward to going to work. Unofficially Denis took me under his wing, and I soaked up everything I could from him. After work we'd all sit in the kitchen and have a few beers, or in Denis' case rum and cokes, and tell stories. It took me a while to figure it out, but one night in that kitchen I realised what it was. I could trust these blokes with anything. I didn't have to look over my shoulder anymore. I was finally with a team of cops who were fair dinkum.

BACK TO THE ROYAL EXCHANGE

By the early 1980s the stream of heroin coming into Australia had become a raging torrent. And because of the competitive market, the purity of street quality heroin had increased significantly. When I was undercover and buying street level deals, the percentage of heroin to the usual additives of baby milk powder, laxative etc. was between three and ten per cent. By the time I was transferred to Taringa, it was closer to twenty. This meant that addicts weren't used to the increased purity and their bodies couldn't cope. People were dying of overdoses in droves.

'Banksy, Denis, job at the RE. There's another OD in the toilets.' Bob had come into the kitchen, where we were making a cup of tea. The Royal Exchange Hotel was on High Street, Toowong. It was an old Victorian-style pub with arched windows and a balcony with filigree metalwork located across the road from the train station.

It was in that beer garden a few years earlier where my cover had almost been blown when a target checked with a contact in the Main Roads department and discovered I was using false number plates. I'd been able to bluff my way out of that by threatening violence and calling him a dog. I was working alone, and that situation had terrified me. But as frightening as it was, the rush of adrenaline was addictive. I missed it.

'Mate, I haven't been to the RE for years.' I looked at Denis. 'Last time I was there I was scoring drugs. Looks like not much has changed.'

Denis stirred his tea. 'Lot of uni students drink there now. The licensee and his son are good blokes and they're trying to clean the place up. I'll introduce you.'

We parked in the rear car park and walked inside. The beer garden looked the same, although deserted at that time of day before the pub had opened. A uniform cop from the Toowong station was standing talking with an older man in his sixties.

'G'day, Denis', said the older man. Denis introduced us. 'Russell, this is Keith. He's new to the office. Keith, this is Russell the licensee.' I shook his hand and introduced myself to the uniform cop. Russell pointed to the male toilets just off the beer garden. 'Another one, third in two months,' he said. 'He must have come in the back just after we opened the doors.'

Denis and I opened the door and walked inside. The urinals were against the wall and two cubicles were to the left. My eyes were drawn to graffiti scrawled above one of the urinals. 'Max Capacity owns a fucking lot of trucks!' University humour.

One of the cubicle doors was propped open and the body of a young man dressed in old jeans, runners and a T-shirt was slumped on the floor on his side. I could see the needle in his arm and the tourniquet still around his bicep. His face was partially obscured due to the angle at which he had fallen. Looking at that kid lying on the dirty floor in a pub toilet, my mind flashed back to a house in Palm Beach in 1980. I was undercover, pretending to be a dealer from Brisbane buying heroin from a network on the Coast, and watched two women inject a young man with his first hit of heroin. I'd thought he was eighteen. I later found out he was fourteen and that first hit was the beginning of a battle with heroin that killed him four years later. He'd also died in a pub toilet with a spike in his arm. This kid was about eighteen. I was hit by a wave of guilt and sadness.

Denis looked at me. 'You alright, mate?'

I nodded and quietly said my mantra for dealing with dead bodies. 'It's not a person anymore, it's just a shell.' This was my way of coping. If I'd let myself think of the person, his family, his hopes and dreams, his unfulfilled life, I would not have been able to do my job.

That afternoon Denis and I went back to the RE, to the lounge bar, for a few beers. I told him the story of Shane, the young kid on the Coast and his death from an overdose. And the guilt I felt because I couldn't intervene. I talked about how Larry and I had been approached to sell heroin for a crew of Drug Squad detectives and about operations where I'd seen the hand of corruption driving the tiller. I told him of seeing some of those detectives bagging up seized dope to sell and how I couldn't trust anyone beyond my undercover circle. Denis was a good listener. A few beers turned into a few hours. 'You don't need to worry about that shit anymore, mate,' he said. 'You're with us now. Another beer?'

I came to know the licensee Russell and his son David very well during my time at Taringa. They were both genuine people who helped us in any way they could. In return, we made sure the police paid appropriate attention to the pub and its surrounds. It became very quickly known that the RE was no longer open for drug business. Over the next few months, the clientele in the beer garden changed from drug dealers and their cohort to university students and theirs. It also became one of my favourite haunts.

WELCOME TO THE OFFICE

As well as his unique manner of keeping his detectives on their toes, Bob Dallow had an interesting way of encouraging less than cooperative offenders to be truthful. I first saw this when I had a prolific break and enter merchant in my office and was trying to persuade him to cooperate and clear up all the outstanding house break-ins I knew he'd committed. Peter and I had executed a search warrant that morning and found a lot of stolen property in his flat. We then collected all the incident reports that listed the same method of breaking in, which was the use of a pipe wrench to jemmy open sliding doors, compared the reports with the stolen property we'd recovered and identified the houses we knew he was right for.

The offender was sitting opposite me with his back to our open office door. He was in his twenties, skinny with lank hair pulled back into a ponytail. Although he had a substantial criminal history of similar offences, he was denying any involvement in any matters that weren't linked to the property we'd found in his flat. 'Mate, you and I both know what you've done. If you tell us now, we can combine the lot and you can do your sentence in one hit. If you don't, I'll pinch you again and you'll get more time.' This was an age-old dance between cop and crook. I knew that he'd ultimately come to the party, but apparently this tactic wasn't paying off quickly enough for Bob.

Suddenly I heard Denis yelling. 'No Boss, no. Don't do it!' The offender spun around in his chair and I looked up from my notes. We both saw the same thing and both of us reacted the same way, with fear and alarm tinged with disbelief.

Bob Dallow had rolled his eyes far back in his head so you could see only the whites of his eyes. A good party trick certainly, but when combined with the butcher's knife he held aloft in his meaty fist and the screams of 'I'll fucking kill him', it was terrifying. When Bob lurched into the office like Frankenstein's monster, Denis grabbed his hand with the knife and dragged him out of sight. 'It's okay, Boss,' he said in soothing tones. 'I'll get your tablets, come on, come with me and sit down. It's okay, he'll tell the truth.' We watched in stunned silence.

The offender turned to me, his eyes wide and his face pale. I probably looked the same. Peter, who had been sitting beside me, shrugged and said, 'The boss doesn't like it when people lie to us. What can I say?' Within the hour, we had cleaned up every break and enter where a pipe wrench had been used and had identified where the stolen property had been fenced.

Bob was a smart leader, so when one of the crew was transferred to another office, he asked if any of us could recommend someone. I knew just the bloke.

Steve Grant had been an undercover operative in the Break and Enter Squad at the same time I was working undercover with the Drug Squad. He and I were now sharing a unit in Toowong, overlooking both reaches of the Brisbane River. We were great mates and I saw a perfect opportunity to bring him on board. I spoke to Bob and shortly after Steve was transferred to Taringa from the City CIB.

Steve was a year or so older than me. At over 182 centimetres, he was fit and had a mop of curly brown hair. He held a second dan in karate and, like me, was a member of the Emergency Squad, the part-time tactical weapons team. He was also in my most trusted circle of undercovers, current and former. And even though I was enjoying working at Taringa, it would be good to have one of my mates there with me. My paranoia had not completely gone away, it was just taking a break, and I would be happier working with someone I knew.

As a courtesy, Steve decided to drop into the office and introduce himself to the boss on the Friday afternoon before he was due to commence. I was out of the office on a job, so wasn't there to warn him about Bob's unique welcome. I met him later at the RE to have a few drinks before we moved on to the Police Club. He had a table waiting for us in the beer garden and was ready to tell me about his afternoon.

Bob had been sitting behind his desk when Steve arrived and introduced himself to Kerry, the public servant at the reception desk. Bob emerged from his office, with his trademark beaming smile. 'Keith's told me about you, mate,' he said. 'Good to have you on board.' They go to the kitchen and Bob makes them coffee. Back in his office and leaning forward in his chair, Bob tells Steve that everyone in his crew is a self-starter. 'Duds don't last long here.'

Steve looks at me earnestly. 'Then as things are winding up, he stands up and looks over my shoulder. He says, "Can I help you, sir?" As I look around, he's leaning forward, and fucking punching me in the chest. He knocked me out of my chair!' The next thing Steve saw was Bob leaning over him with that beaming smile. Helping Steve up, Bob repeats his mantra: 'None of my detectives gets sucked in like that. Welcome to Taringa.'

'That's Bob's way of saying he likes you,' I say. 'Be careful, mate, he'll try it on any time . . . Oh, and he also has this thing he does with a butcher's knife.'

TARINGA TERRORS

I'd been at Taringa for a few months when my detective designation was confirmed. I now held the rank of one of the best jobs in the Queensland Police, a detective senior constable. Not too much responsibility, the ability to work relatively unsupervised and still spend most of the time on the road locking up bad guys. I asked Bob to approve partnering me with Steve and to my great surprise he agreed.

We were both keen and active young cops who still thought the Job was serious, and we thrived on chasing crooks. That was the plus side. The other side of the ledger was that neither of us was committed to following rules, including wearing ties and having regulation haircuts, staying within our division and generally behaving ourselves. We would have been bloody difficult to manage but I think Bob was so happy with our arrest activity that he didn't care about the rest. In fact, I think he liked that fact that we were not your usual kind of cop.

One afternoon he received a phone call from a detective inspector at CIB headquarters. Steve and I had been there to obtain files about some of the crooks we were working on and to flirt with the female public servants. We strolled into the office laughing and joking when Bob's voice stopped us in our tracks. 'You two clowns, in my office. NOW!'

'What the fuck have we done now?' I whispered to Steve. 'No idea,' was the reply.

We walked into Bob's office like whipped cattle dogs with our tails between our legs. His face was set and angry. 'I've just had a phone call from Detective Inspector Pointing at CIB headquarters. He was pretty pissed off that you were in there without ties.'

My eyes immediately fell to Bob's open shirt collar, a place I rarely saw a tie. I thought the better of pointing this out and poking what appeared to be a very angry bear. 'This is an official direction,' he continued. 'Next time you go into headquarters for any reason, you are to wear a tie. Understood?'

'Yes, boss,' we replied in unison, like two schoolboys in front of the principal.

'And these are the ties you are going to wear. Take your pick.' With that Bob closed his office door where ten or so of the ugliest ties I had ever seen were hanging. They were wide and loud, adorned with cartoon characters and beach scenes. To top it off, an elastic loop allowed each tie to be simply slipped over the head.

Bob looked at us. 'I fucking hate ties,' he said, breaking out into his infectious laugh. 'Let's see how long they want you to wear a tie after this.'

The man was a genius. Within a week he received another phone call, 'Tell Banks and Grant not to come in here with those ties again. I don't bloody care what they wear.'

Steve and I were named the Taringa Terrors by the other detectives, a moniker that applied more to our irreverent attitudes than our arrest activity, and we certainly managed live up to it. We were the youngest in the office, by age and attitudinally, but we also had the energy that youth brings. We volunteered for every early morning raid and job that had the promise of action and the chance to go hands on with crooks. We enjoyed nothing more than rough and tumble policing and would race to any job in or out of our division. That's how we came to be the first detectives on the scene of a murder about 20 kilometres away from our office.

It was a quiet Friday night in our area, so we decided to take a drive into the city and maybe have a quiet beer or two. On the way, an urgent call went out. 'VKR to any unit in the Nundah area, a male person reports he has killed his partner.' We looked at each other. Neither of us had charged anyone with murder yet. 'Go mate go' was all the encouragement Steve needed. He promptly did his best to break the land speed record from Auchenflower to Nundah.

I have no idea how long the drive took us, but we pulled up in a scream of brakes outside the address. There were already two or three marked police cars on site. We went straight inside. A junior uniformed constable stood facing a man in his late twenties who was sitting on a three-seater lounge facing a television set. He was holding a wine glass and an opened cask of chardonnay sat on the low coffee table in front of him. To his right, I saw the body of another man lying face down on the floor.

'G'day, mate, Detectives Banks and Grant. You okay?' He looked up at us, took a drink and calmly answered, 'I killed him. I strangled him and I'd do it again.'

The uniformed cop was young and looked believable (juries loved young, uniformed cops), so I needed him to make notes of the admission to support our evidence. (In those days, before the use of tape-recorded evidence, it was common at trials for defence counsel to say, 'I put it to you that this conversation with my client never happened and was invented by you'.)

Steve had his notebook out and delivered the required caution to the man, telling him that he did not have to answer any of our questions. 'Yes gorgeous,' the man replied gazing adoringly at Steve, who was a good-looking bloke. 'I told him and told him how much I loved watching *Blankety Blanks*. Graham Kennedy does a wonderful Cyril. But he turned the channel once too fucking often. So I hit him with the ashtray.' The man pointed with his chin at a heavy glass ashtray on the floor beside the body. 'Then I strangled him. When I thought he was dead, I got a glass of wine. Care for one?' he asked.

We both shook our heads.

'So then I turned the TV back to *Blankety Blanks* and he started gurgling. So, I strangled him again and made sure he was dead. Bastard.'

Steve was furiously writing in his notebook when the front door opened and in walked two Homicide Squad detectives. They were dressed in the normal CIB attire of business trousers, white shirts and dark ties, and black shoes. 'Thanks, boys, we'll take it from here,' one of them announced dismissively. 'Leave your names with the uniforms.'

I looked back at him, 'No problems, boys, we'll just take our notes of the admissions he's made with us then.'

As we got back into the car Steve asked, 'How much do you like *Blankety Blanks*?' I thought about it. 'A lot, so I'd be careful about changing the channel without asking if I was you.'

We didn't manage to make the arrest for murder, but we were recorded as assisting and that was almost as good. In fact, it deserved a celebratory beer. And strangely, no questions were asked about being out of our division.

EVIL

Television and movies paint a picture of police work as being all about car chases, shoot outs and crimes solved by brilliant deduction. The reality is that it is mostly procedural, a hard slog following lines of inquiry and tip offs, and involves a lot of paperwork, although that paperwork is now digital. Thankfully, most police never fire their weapon at another person, at least not in this country.

But the Job can be dangerous. The real and present danger for every police officer is the unrelenting emotional damage of dealing with people at their worst, victims and offenders. I defy anyone to walk in the shoes of police in the real world and walk away unaffected. Post-traumatic stress disorder is not only caused by extreme events of life-threatening danger, but it also accumulates over years of dealing with the darkness and evil in people.

The other certainty of policing is that nothing is predictable and that some things, once experienced, are impossible to forget.

That was the case at 9.30 one morning as I was sitting behind the reception desk with Kerry, the station public servant. when a woman in her mid- to late thirties walked through the door. She was holding the hand of a girl, who looked about twelve or thirteen, dressed in a school uniform.

'Good morning, how can I help you?' I asked.

'I want to report that my daughter has been sexually assaulted,' She replied. I looked at the girl clutching her mother's hand. She was almost as tall as her mother and stood with her eyes downcast.

I lifted the counter flap and asked them to come in. Kerry took the girl to her desk and I showed the woman to one at the other end of the office. I made her a cup of tea. What she told me has never left me.

She had remarried when her daughter was seven years old. They lived in the beautiful nearby suburb of Kenmore. Her new husband was the manager of a small transport business and he had quickly become close to her daughter, lavishing her with attention. 'I didn't know what was happening until this morning when I was putting on washing and found blood in her underwear,' she said, tears welling in her eyes. 'She told me everything. That bastard started raping her when she was nine. The blood was from last night when he raped her anally.'

I felt a surge of rage. I found it hard to maintain my professional and emotional distance. I wanted to find this bastard and tear his head off but had to swallow my anger. An expert female detective from the Sexual Offences Squad took over the case and the woman and her daughter were taken to the Royal Brisbane Hospital, where the girl underwent the required medical examinations.

'If you want to pinch this bastard, he's all yours,' Bob said. 'You just need to understand that all the allegations must be put to him and you can't touch him. If you do, that can fuck up the trial. I'm not saying he doesn't deserve a flogging, but you can't.'

'I can't promise that, Bob. You didn't see that little girl. I know my limitations. If I'm in a room with him, I won't be able to keep my hands to myself.'

'I understand, mate, I've got kids. If it was my daughter, I'd fucking kill him.'

Bob knew this one had affected me badly. He had me brief the two to ten shift and they took over.

By the time the husband was brought back for the formal interview, Steve and I were at the RE and I was trying to drink enough to forget what I'd heard that morning. But alcohol doesn't drown your problems, it just makes them swim. 'I'm going back to the office, I announced. 'I want to see what this arsehole looks like'.

Steve shook his head. 'Not a good idea, mate.' He knew I was more than capable of violence; we'd had our fair share of going hands on with those stupid enough to resist arrest.

'Well, I'll see you at home then.'

'Nope; if you're going, I'm coming with you.'

There were no formal interview rooms at Taringa. We came in via the back door and heard a voice from one of the rooms. An afternoon shift detective was conducting a formal interview. 'So, you told us you've been having consensual sex with your step-daughter for some time. Can you tell us if you have ever had anal sex with her?' he asked.

As a male voice answered. 'Yep. I told you boys she came on to me. I want that on the record. So last night she asked me to fuck her in the arse. You've seen her, how could I say no?' I could hear his words being typed up by the detective.

I said nothing, but knew what I wanted to do to him. Before I could take a step, Steve had me in a vice-like bear hug. He dragged me out of the office and down the stairs. I had never felt such murderous rage. By the time we were back at the RE, I had calmed down. I was drained and exhausted. I looked at Steve. 'Thanks, mate. I guess that shows I don't have a future working in Child Abuse. I'd end up killing one of the bastards. Fuck it, let's get pissed.'

Months later at the Police Club, I ran into the detective who'd interviewed the girl and taken her statement. I bought her a drink to say thanks. 'I don't know how you can do this work,' I said. 'I couldn't handle it. I take my hat off to you guys.'

'I have to get out. It's fucked me up too much,' she said, looking up at me with immense sadness. 'I've seen so much that I can't have sex with my husband anymore without having these horrible images flash in my mind. I've got to get out.' And that's what she did a little while later, when she handed in her resignation.

There was little emotional support for anyone in the Job in those days. The dangers of police work weren't just about the violence we saw and experienced. They were much more than that and the scars were not always visible. It was considered weak in a culture where strength was valued to admit you were having problems dealing with the things you saw, so you just kept it to yourself. That's why there were so many broken marriages and more than a few suicides. For many police, the pub was their church.

THE LIST

There is a truism that the people you meet in the Job are either the best people you will ever know or the biggest idiots and there's no grey area in between. Fortunately, the good people far outweigh the idiots but too often the idiots are placed in roles they probably shouldn't be in.

Life went on for Steve and me. We worked well together and had fun doing so. But, as we all know, the universe has a habit of throwing things our way that we don't see coming. One morning Steve and I were in the office doing paperwork when a uniformed senior constable named Gary dropped in from the Toowong station for a chat. There was nothing unusual about that, the crew at Taringa had developed an excellent working relationship with all uniform stations in our division. Unlike most CIB area offices, we helped them with investigations and arrests rather than take them away, unless they were matters we needed to handle such as rape, robbery and the like. I took Gary into my office.

'Mate,' he said quietly, 'you need to know this. There's a crew in the JAB [Juvenile Aid Bureau] that has the job of putting together files on gay coppers. One of them was on the piss in the club and boasting to a few people that you're on the list.' He named the detective. I knew him, but not well. I'd seen him glaring at me on some

Friday nights at the Police Club and I was starting to understand why.

'Is that right?'

I wasn't too surprised. I'd been called gay by some redneck cops every now and then since Academy days. It was a favourite insult, mostly by cops who fell into the biggest idiot category. I was probably placed on the file because of an undercover operation at the Alliance Hotel a few years before. The Alliance was the home of a leather bar, part of the underground gay scene. I'd assumed the cover of a gay man who wanted to buy drugs. Big deal. I wasn't bothered by small-minded homophobic morons. To be honest, I'd been more affronted a couple of years earlier when a particularly loud-mouthed detective sergeant at the Break and Enter Squad had proclaimed, 'You must be a fucking pommy, the way you talk.' Having been raised in the Queensland outback and being an avowed republican, that was a much bigger insult than being called gay.

There had been rumours that the police commissioner, Terry Lewis, was obsessed with identifying gay police, which was interesting because he later tried to protect Senior Constable Dave Moore, who'd been charged with soliciting underage boys for sex. Moore was the face of the Queensland Police on a Channel 7 Saturday morning kids' show where he had a regular slot. He was sentenced to two and a half years imprisonment.

The JAB had been Lewis' project and it had been instrumental in addressing juvenile crime. But now it appeared that the bureau was being used for another, more insidious project. It was also rumoured that Assistant Commissioner Tony Murphy had an interest, but his motives were darker, in that he could use the information to black-mail influential people, including politicians and some senior police. Being gay in those days meant you could be manipulated.

'Don't worry about it, mate. It's because I don't wear cheap brown pants, nylon shirts and white socks. Anyone who doesn't dress that way is likely to be gay in his world.' It probably didn't help that I still wore an earring off duty, one legacy of my undercover life that I kept hold of.

'Careful, mate,' I said to Steve, who was listening. 'You'll be next with those snappy suits you wear to court.'

'Fuck 'em,' he laughed.

Gary lowered his voice. 'That's not all. He says you're a paedophile.'

When I'm angry I don't yell or pound the table. I just stood and nodded slowly. 'Thanks, Gary,' I said very quietly and deliberately before turning to Steve. 'I need to go to the city and see someone.'

Gripped by a cold fury, I signed out one of the station cars but just as I was putting the key in the door, I saw Bob and Steve hurry down the stairs. Bob was clear and calm. 'Keith, come back inside. I'll sort this out. No one fucks with my men.' I badly wanted to punch the fuck out of the clown at JAB but I respected Bob. I went back inside. He sat me down. 'You're one of my detectives. I told you that on the first day. I'll look after this. If I have to, I'll fucking bash him myself. Steve, take him to the pub.'

The next day Bob told me it was sorted. I believed him, too. He was the last man a JAB detective would want to see angry.

Years later I discovered the JAB had been investigating child abuse, particularly the activities of police and public servants in organised paedophile rings. I applaud the investigation and I'm sure the detectives in that team would have followed lines of investigation based on more than how someone dressed. Even after all these years, it still angers me that such a small-minded man with a narrow view of the world could have ruined my life.

In 1998 an inquiry headed by Justice Kimmins was established into allegations of police misconduct during the investigation of paedophilia in Queensland. It was launched after the *Courier Mail* ran several stories alleging Lewis' interference with paedophile investigations. I'm not able to comment on the accuracy or otherwise of those allegations, but what interested me was that the inquiry heard that Lewis maintained dirt files on police and prominent figures during his tenure as police commissioner and that these files were kept in a locked safe at the JAB. Some JAB detectives, concerned about potential interference in their investigations by senior police, broke into the locked safe and copied files for their personal safekeeping. Ultimately the inquiry sensationally found no evidence to support any of the allegations.

Perhaps my name was on another file, one that disappeared during the tsunami that was the Fitzgerald Inquiry, or perhaps it was just a matter of a drunken cop boasting about what he could do to me if he wanted to. Whatever the truth, that detective never knew how close he came to a broken jaw, which would not have been a good outcome for either of us.

———

I know that some retired and former police officers describe Commissioner Lewis as the best boss we ever had. They talk nostalgically about being allowed to have two beers on a meal break; how promotion was by seniority; how police weren't hamstrung by as many rules as they are today; and how they policed the streets better then. I once disagreed with those views but am now more accepting. A lot of police weren't exposed to the corruption I saw so they look at that era through a different lens.

The reality was, though, that your career could be destroyed by others and you might never know why. Like a friend who was transferred overnight from Brisbane to Cooktown over 1900 kilometres away. His crime? A speeding ticket for Russell Hinze, a powerful minister in Bjelke-Petersen's government. Hinze pulled out a map of Queensland and said, 'Pick somewhere, son. You'll be transferred there tomorrow.' At least he had a choice, I guess. Others ended up in far-flung towns without any recourse or appeal.

But that era offered far worse than an unwanted transfer. Large stations became dumping grounds for men who had serious drinking problems, and spent their shifts pissed. If they stayed in the job and didn't die, they were guaranteed promotion under the good bloke rule and put in charge of serious cops who wanted to protect the public. Putting aside the corruption and cover-ups, the overwhelming majority of police were committed to protecting the public from criminals. But we were under-paid and under-resourced. Our equipment was sub-standard and we weren't supported by proper legislation. Give me a break. Things under Commissioner Lewis weren't all rainbows and unicorns.

BATTLE WING

I had the best of both worlds. I was working as a detective in a busy office with a great bunch of people and I was also at the sharp end, training in special weapons and tactics, through my participation in the Emergency Squad. That was where the fun was.

In 1982, not long after I'd gone back to uniform, I'd seen television coverage of a domestic siege on the Gold Coast. The response had included heavily armed police from the Emergency Squad. The siege was resolved peacefully but, once I saw the footage of cops dressed in black carrying Armalite M16 rifles, I was hooked. I wanted to be one of those guys.

The Queensland Police Emergency Squad had been established sometime in the 1960s to deal with siege situations and high-risk police operations. By 1982 it comprised fifty officers drawn from various uniformed areas and the CIB. All members were part time and were only called out when needed. I submitted a written application, was interviewed and accepted as a trainee.

On my first training day with the squad at a rifle range, I met another young cop named Peter Kidd. He was a month or two older than me and his enthusiasm was infectious. 'This is the future, mate,' he said. 'One day this will be a permanent squad and I'm going to be part of it.' His words were prophetic, but his prediction wouldn't be fulfilled for another five years.

I looked at him, 'Mate, I'll be right beside you,' and we shook hands on it.

On that sunny Brisbane day, at a rifle range with the smell of cordite heavy in the air, neither of us could have foretold how our lives would be intertwined and what fate held in store for us. All that mattered was that we were both part of a squad that did what other police couldn't. We were young and in our prime, and that was good enough.

It was perfect timing because that year Brisbane would be hosting the Commonwealth Games and the Queensland Police Force had received an injection of federal funding as part of a national counter terrorist initiative. That meant new toys. Previously the squad had trained with Vietnam War era weapons: 7.62 calibre self-loading rifles (SLRs), 5.56 calibre M16 Armalite rifles, pump action shotguns and sniper rifles. In 1982 we had deliveries of new Israeli Uzi and German Heckler and Koch sub-machine guns, advanced sniper rifles, .357 Magnum handguns, gas masks, black coveralls designed for tactical work, tear gas guns and so on. As a young man looking for excitement this was the next thing to heaven.

We trained four days per month at various Army locations, as well as at civilian rifle ranges. We were trained in how to strip, assemble and fire the various weapons. We also learned how to rappel (abseil) down the steep cliffs of volcanic rock at Kangaroo Point with views to the CBD directly across the expanse of the Brisbane River. On some training days we'd travel to an abandoned quarry near the western suburb of Mitchelton and learn forward-rappelling over the sheer sides of the quarry. Only weeks out from the 1982 Commonwealth Games, helicopter insertions became a part of the counter terrorist responses we were practising.

Just after sunset one night, four of us were standing on the landing skids of an RAAF 9 Squadron Iroquois helicopter cruising at around eight hundred feet. We were flying towards an abandoned four-storey building we were using in a training exercise. I could see the lights of Ipswich in the distance. The rotor blades' distinctive *wop wop* sound, familiar to thousands of Vietnam War veterans, cut through the night.

My life depended on the rope that fed through my rappelling harness to a metal fixture on the floor of the chopper. This was probably my tenth jump, but I still held the rope with a white-knuckle death grip. I was conscious of the weight of the submachine gun secured on its three-point sling across the Kevlar vest over my chest. As we approached the building the pilot guided the helicopter to hover some twelve metres above the rooftop. The crew chief gave the signal to go and all four of us fell deliberately backwards and smoothly rappelled downwards. As we landed on the roof, we unhooked our ropes, reattached other ropes ready to go, moved to the edge of the building and ran face down to the ground. We were standing together beside the building entrance waiting for our turn to do it again, our blood pumping, when Peter grinned at me and said, 'How good is this, mate? And we get paid to do it!' I couldn't wipe the smile off my face.

——

Each year the Emergency Squad spent twelve days straight training at the Land Warfare Centre, Canungra, a training area steeped in rich Army tradition. Located in the Gold Coast hinterland among thick rainforest and steep razor back country, Canungra was established in 1942 to train troops to be deployed to the Pacific theatre because it best replicated the jungle environment of the Pacific region. Later generations of Australian soldiers, including those deployed to Malaya, Borneo and Vietnam, all underwent training at Canungra as well. The entire area comprises about 6000 hectares.

We spent most of our time under the control of Army staff attached to Battle Wing, Canungra and during our first camp we learned navigation, slogging through the jungle with its lantana and intense vegetation. We also undertook obstacle courses and day and night shooting practice, and completed the notorious confidence course well known to all ADF veterans of that time, which was an obstacle course on steroids. We were barracked four to a room and ate our meals in the Sergeants Mess when we weren't in the field. After dinner we went to the Snake Pit, the name given to the bar and beer garden in the Sergeants Mess adjoining the silver service dining room. We mixed with Vietnam veterans, men hardened by their experience in that war. I was in my element.

When the first camp finished, we were confirmed as squad members and presented with gold lapel badges embossed with the initials E.S. to be worn on our uniform collars. We then embarked on an accelerated training program to prepare for the Games, including learning how to rappel from a helicopter as a rapid deployment in the event of a terrorist incident.

The Emergency Squad was deployed to the Police Academy on standby for the duration of the Games. Two 9 Squadron RAAF Iroquois helicopters were located on the football oval ready to move but, like us, they sat unneeded for the ten days of the Games.

Even though we spent our days at the Academy in a state of boredom, accreditation gave us unfettered access to the entire

Games village. On our days and nights off, we could be found in the athletes' village. More specifically we could be found at the athletes' bar, meeting many of the competitors and doing our bit to foster international relations.

I stayed as a part-time member of the Emergency Squad while working full time as a junior detective. The squad was predominantly called out for domestic sieges and, in a time when high-powered rifles were easily available in stores, these callouts became frequent. Most sieges were resolved by negotiation, but occasionally a team was sent in to smash down the door. Amazingly, and thankfully, no shots were ever fired on these callouts, whether planned raids or sieges. It was something I hadn't really thought about, but I was confident I could squeeze the trigger if I had to.

I couldn't wait for Peter Kidd's vison of a full-time squad to come true; this was where the action would be.

JUST IN CASE

In the early to mid-1980s violence against police was common, but the use of guns against cops was rare. That was changing, however. High-powered rifles and pump-action shotguns were legally available in thousands of stores, not just gun shops, across Australia. The black market in illegal handguns was going gangbusters. Armed robberies were increasing and in Sydney police were being shot at more and more often. For any cop who could read the environment, it was time to start getting serious about tactics and training, just in case. It was still not mandatory to carry a gun on duty in Queensland, but more and more of us were thinking it was better to carry one and not need it than to need one and not have it. I'd been carrying one since having a shotgun thrust in my face during a domestic dispute when I had barely four weeks' service.

On 10 October 1981, Mobile Patrol crews had been in a high-speed chase pursuing a murder suspect from the murder scene when he drove his car through the plate glass windows of the entrance to the Royal Brisbane Hospital, stopping inside the foyer. Armed with a high-powered rifle and, sheltering behind his car, the offender fired numerous shots at the pursuing police. Police returned his fire, and the gunman was wounded. He then killed himself with his own rifle.

The problem was that some of the cops were using department-issued Smith and Wesson .38 revolvers loaded with department-issued bullets, known as wadcutters. Wadcutters were designed to leave a nice round hole in a paper target, and not for use in a close quarter gun battle. The police could see their bullets strike the rear windshield of the offender's car and bounce off.

One of Commissioner Terry Lewis' initiatives had been to allow members of the Queensland Police Pistol Club to purchase and carry their own firearms on duty up to and including .357 Magnum revolvers. I doubt this was anything more than a cost saving measure but, whatever the reason, it paid off. Two of the police in the hospital shoot out were carrying their own .357 revolvers, with their own purchased ammunition. I have no doubt had they not been armed that night with guns firing ammunition capable of wounding the offender, then police would have died. They were all brave men who went above and beyond, but it was bloody good luck they hadn't ended up in police coffins as a result of poor equipment, under-resourcing and a casual approach to officer safety.

Incidents like this were another reason I wanted to be prepared, mentally and physically, and have the best training I could find. If I ever had to react in a gun battle, I wanted to be completely ready.

I had known Speedy since my first deployment at Mobiles and met Wendy when I went back there for a while after undercover. They were both good street cops and were tactically aware in their interactions with offenders. There was no officer survival training provided to police in the 1980s and the only way to get information was to read police magazines and journals from the United States. Both Speedy and Wendy had been heavily influenced in their approach to street tactics by the Royal Brisbane Hospital shoot out. Speedy had also been a member of the Police Pistol Club since 1978 and carried a .357 Colt Python six-shot revolver. He'd schooled himself in officer survival tactics used in vehicle stops and other high-risk activities while Wendy utilised her tactical experience from ten years in the Army Reserve. They frequently discussed scenarios and what their responses would be. Just in case . . .

1.00 am, 29 October 1983

Wendy was bored. She and Speedy had been permanent partners at Mobiles for two years and their patrol area was Mt Gravatt and surrounding suburbs on the south side. Both were in their twenties and, like a lot of Mobiles cops, loved doing police work, the more exciting the better. But night work wasn't always busy. Boredom was often the catalyst for trouble.

Wendy looked at Speedy. 'Nothing happening here, what say we go out and poach somewhere?'

'Caesars is always good,' Speedy grinned. 'A UIL [under the influence of liquor] is better than nothing, and you never know what they might have in the car.' Drink driving was almost a national sport in the 1980s.

They both figured that while they weren't supposed to leave their defined patrol area, all would be forgiven if they picked up an arrest.

Caesars Palace was a stand-alone nightclub located in Logan Road, Underwood. It was a classy establishment with amateur strip nights (for both ladies and gentlemen, the management was ahead of its time for gender equality), live bands, brawls (amateur of course) and various other drawcards for the locals. The only thing missing was a wire cage, Blues Brothers-style, to protect the band on stage.

Speedy and Wendy travelled down Logan Road away from Upper Mt Gravatt, past the Big Gun shopping centre, which, like a lot in Queensland, was named without guile or hidden meaning. It literally had a big artillery piece in the car park. As they neared the garish, flashing lights marking Caesars Palace, an old model Sigma sedan pulled out of a side street about a hundred metres in front of them.

'No tail-lights, what a genius,' Speedy observed dryly. 'We'd better get to him before a truck smashes into him.'

They sped up and activated the blue light and hit the siren. 'Five occupants,' said Wendy. 'You take the driver; I'll do the watching from the left rear.'

The car pulled over and Speedy walked up to the driver, shining his Maglite torch inside. 'G'day, mate, driver's licence, please. Who owns the car?'

The driver, a young male, looked up at him. 'I don't know.' Speedy opened the driver's door. 'Hop out of the car please.' He leant down and spoke to the others. 'You blokes stay where you are.'

Speedy and the driver walked to the boot as Wendy kept an eye on the others. 'No tail-lights, mate, you could've been hit by one of those transport trucks. The truckie wouldn't have seen you. Where are you going?'

The driver looked troubled. 'The Coast. Shit, I had no idea about the lights.'

Speedy opened the boot and looked at the tail-lights for signs of damage. 'We'll need to check the fuse box. Who owns this bag?' He pointed to a black backpack in the boot.

'The bloke in the passenger seat, only met him tonight at Caesars. He said that he was off to the Coast and asked if we wanted to come with him. He gave me the keys.'

Speedy looked at Wendy and with that unspoken language understood by permanent partners, she knew he wanted the bag checked. Wendy went to the front passenger side and opened the door. 'That your bag in the boot, mate?'

The passenger looked at her, unconcerned. 'Sure is, you need to have a look?'

Wendy stepped back to allow him to climb out and replied, 'Yes thanks. Just go to the back of the car please.' She followed him to the rear of the car and stopped to keep an eye on him as Speedy opened the bag. The driver was back in the driver's seat.

Wendy kept the passenger in her view as the bag was searched. 'Anything in here you need to tell us about?' she asked.

'No, nothing at all, just some clothes,' he replied unfazed.

'Nothing in here hey? What about this?' asked Speedy, picking up a foil package lying at the top of the unzipped bag.

Wendy turned her head and felt the man's firm grip on her arm. She brought up her other hand and the Maglite torch only to see the barrel of a revolver millimetres from her face.

In times of extreme stress, the mind operates at a different level. Every detail is in focus and time slows down. For Wendy, all that she saw was the large black hole of the muzzle. It filled her vision. Escape scenarios played rapid fire in her mind.

In those seconds, Speedy also considered his options. He knew he could draw and fire into the man's head. He was one of the best shots in the department, but he was also acutely aware of the situation they were in. 'All I could think of was that if I shot him, he'd still be able to pull the trigger and he couldn't miss from where he was. Wendy would be dead. I did the next best thing; I threw my hands up in the air like some cowboy in a Western movie. I was hoping that the cars driving past would see me in obvious danger and call the police.'

'Put your hands down and turn around,' the man demanded. He kept hold of Wendy, pressing the gun against her temple and pushing her sideways to stand behind Speedy. Keeping the gun against her head, he took Speedy's .357 from his holster.

In those days, policewomen were not allowed to wear visible firearms and certainly not a utility belt. Appearance over safety! They were issued with a handbag in which they were expected to carry their revolver, baton, handcuffs, notebook and so on. Wendy, however, was wearing an ankle holster with her .38 Smith and Wesson secured by a thumb snap clip and loaded with .38 +P hollow point bullets. 'My mind was frantically going through scenarios,' she reflected later. '*Can I distract him to get to my gun? Can I pretend to faint and get to it that way? Can I hit him somehow?* But by now, he had two guns and both were pointed at us.'

The man snarled at the driver, 'Get out of the fucking car and get my bag out of the front seat.'

Petrified, the driver stammered to Wendy, 'What should I do?'

She looked at him, 'Get the fucking bag and do what he says.'

The driver retrieved a black sports bag from the front passenger foot well and stood up.

'Put it in the cop car,' the man instructed. Then he put the small revolver he was holding in his pocket and transferred Speedy's Colt Python to his right hand and held it to Wendy's head. He looked at Speedy. 'Don't do anything stupid.'

The man moved Wendy to the front passenger seat of the police car and sat in the driver's seat. Still pointing the gun at her head, he went through her police handbag sitting on the console. She sat with her hands dangling, waiting for a chance to draw her revolver. 'I was certain he was taking me hostage and if he drove away, one of us would die before the ride ended.'

Speedy made sure he stayed in full view, not wanting to take the chance of antagonising the man.

Satisfied, the man told Wendy to get out of the car and close the door. Keeping the gun trained on both of them through the passenger window, he used his left hand to turn the ignition key, started the police car and sped off in a cloud of dust and gravel.

Wendy and Speedy raced to the Sigma and Speedy grabbed the keys from the boot lock. They grabbed the three other passengers in the car and threw them out onto the road. They now had a pursuit car. There was a problem, however: the police car had six cylinders and the Sigma was a four-cylinder manual. No contest really.

The police car did a U-turn, took off at high speed and was gone. Mobile phones didn't exist, and handheld radios weren't issued because they were deemed not necessary. They couldn't call for assistance.

Speedy floored it, and as they neared Caesars Wendy saw a black and white taxi, which she flagged down to use the taxi radio. Within minutes the area was flooded with Mobile patrol cars, traffic cars, detectives and the dog squad. The missing police car was found in the car park of the Kuraby Hotel. Wendy recalled later, 'If we'd caught him, I would have shot him, no doubt. I was literally hanging out of the car window with my gun in my hand.'

The man was found and arrested. An escapee from Sydney's Silverwater gaol, where he had been serving ten years for armed robbery, he'd also been wanted for thirteen armed robberies committed since his escape. As for the bag he retrieved from the car, it contained heroin with a street value of around one million dollars. His destination was Sydney, and he was using the others in the car for cover. Both Wendy and Speedy were struck by how cool and in control he had been. When he was interviewed by the detectives, he told them he'd hit up with heroin a little while beforehand and that was why he was so chilled.

Today both Speedy and Wendy would receive psychological counselling and as much time off as they needed to recover. Instead, they were both interviewed by a detective inspector from Internal Investigations who demanded to know why they were two kilometres outside their defined patrol area.

A few days later during their shift, Speedy mentioned to Wendy he was having bad dreams about that night.

'Yeah, I'm having trouble sleeping too,' she answered.

'That's good, I thought it was just me.'

That was the state of welfare in the Queensland Police in the 'good old days'. You looked after yourself and your partner as best you could. And you went back to work on the street carrying spare ammunition. Just in case.

TOO DEEP, TOO LONG

Larry was happy to see me. 'Want a smoke?'

'No mate, trying to be the straight cop now.' I missed the sweet smell and the pleasant buzz of a spliff but that was the old under-cover life. 'You go ahead though.'

Larry looked tired and jaded, more than I had seen him before. He smiled briefly, 'Nah, I need to cut down anyway. I'll get us a couple of beers.'

I was hanging out at his apartment and his flatmate Kathleen was at work. She was an advertising executive, blonde, petite, full of life and someone who lived in a world far away from criminals and their victims. Larry and Kathleen were old friends and she'd played a part in the recapture of the escapee who had planned to murder Larry and me during our undercover job in Cairns. The guy had been on the run and had called the telephone number of their apartment asking for Larry by his undercover name, and Kathleen had gone along with the ruse. I was impressed by her coolness under pressure and her obvious excitement at being part of something way outside her experience. She was also single and very pretty.

'I'm getting sick of the life, mate,' Larry said. 'All I do is meet people, bullshit, score, bullshit some more, rinse and repeat. I need to get out, but I don't think I can. 'I don't know how you did it, back to uniform, then to the Branch. This is who I am now, and I don't think I could handle the straight life.' I knew what he meant. Thankfully I got out in time.

Larry had started his career like I had. He wanted to be a good cop and do something worthwhile to help change the world, but just like it had with me, the world changed him in ways he never expected. Unlike me, however, he stayed in undercover and was moving further and further away from the gentle, funny and philosophical young man I'd first met. He was hyper vigilant and had an air of anger and violence just lurking beneath the surface. He was one of my closest friends, the older brother I'd never had, and I was worried about him.

'Why not go back to Mobiles, mate? You have good friends there.' But I knew what his answer would be. 'No, KJ, I couldn't handle the hours. I need a job where I can get up at 11 every day.'

I knew Larry had been working as an undercover agent far too long and so had Spider, another close mate who'd started undercover about twelve months after I had. Spider had grown up on the north coast of New South Wales, joined the Queensland Police and before long had volunteered for undercover. On Spider's first day at the Drug Squad, not only did he get his false number plates, his small automatic pistol and a false driver's licence, he'd also been handed a bag of pot. 'This is for you,' he was told with no explanation.

'I took the bag home and put it on my beside table,' he told me. 'It stayed there for a week. I had no idea what I was supposed to do with it. I wasn't a smoker [of pot]. No one told me anything. I thought it might have been some sort of integrity test. Every morning I'd wake up and look at it and wonder what to do with it.'

Within a couple of months, Spider realised that smoking dope was part of the job and he embraced it with relish. Like we all did. The price paid by young undercover officers was that our lives were irrevocably changed. All of us were casualties, some more so than others. Living a double life is not natural for anyone, but the rush and the buzz of lying to drug dealers and busting them was almost impossible to give up. It was a siren song calling from the dark side.

I could see both Larry and Spider changing, and not for the better. Living as drug dealers, even though it was a fake life, was causing major problems. They were too far under to come back to the surface easily. Paranoia, increasing drug and alcohol use and a belief that they could do whatever they wanted became a recipe for disaster, but no one cared too much about the welfare of under-covers, apart from other undercovers.

I had a twinge of anger at being removed from the Drug Squad and not being able to help them, but that anger quickly passed. I was happy at Taringa CIB and no longer on edge. I knew I couldn't change the world. Now that I was away from undercover, I could clearly see how damaging it was. All I could do was to be there for my mates and try to help them remember who they really were, not who they pretended to be.

SILVER LINING

Paperwork was the bane of my existence, and I'm certain I wasn't alone. I seemed to spend most of my time typing up files on minor complaints such as stolen garden gnomes, missing garden hoses, stolen bicycles and a myriad of other petty crimes that would never be solved. We just didn't have time to investigate them, but the bureaucracy needed to have the files closed with the right file number. This was just one of the many tiresome duties of policing.

But the universe provides. Police can be victims of crime as well. One morning Steve and I arrived at the office around eight to be greeted by the sight of a Scenes of Crime officer photographing the door to the exhibit room. 'What's happening, mate?' I asked.

He turned to look at us. 'Someone's helped themselves to your exhibits.' The door had been forced open and the space that had been occupied by large mature cannabis plants the day before was now empty. We'd raided a house a few days before and found half a dozen large plants in the lounge room. The owner had been charged with cultivation and the plants seized, taken to the office and stored pending formal botanic analysis.

'It's not all bad,' I said to Steve. 'They didn't take the fridge.'

Bob was not happy. 'Some bastard has broken in, boys. Check your lockers.'

There was no budget for security alarms in those days. Our lockers had been forced open and I'd lost ammunition, a couple of holsters and a torch. Steve's locker was similarly rifled. It was obvious the burglars had taken their time searching the office. File folders had been strewn on the floor and other items thrown carelessly around the office as they searched for anything valuable.

A little while later, Denis strolled past the kitchen on his way to the backyard incinerator clutching a box of matches. He had a stack of files tucked under his arm. 'You know what I really can't understand?' he asked holding up the matches. 'Why wouldn't they just be happy with stealing exhibits and our property? They also had to steal our paperwork. I'll never understand crooks.'

I looked at the others. 'Guess I'd better check my files too.'

It's true, every cloud has a silver lining.

EVOLUTION

In 1984, the year of the XXIII Summer Olympics, the Emergency Squad enjoyed its last two-week training camp living in barracks and dining in the finery of the Sergeants Mess at Canungra. Each day started with a run or other torture designed by the Army physical training instructors, who should have a little place in hell reserved just for them, followed by breakfast in the beautiful Mess with table service provided by male and female stewards.

The new intake of Emergency Squad trainees spent their two weeks in freezing conditions (I never understood why we couldn't go in summer) under the watchful eye of the Army training staff from Battle Wing. The rest of us trained with the SAS instructors, refining close quarter battle skills on firing ranges and in the killing house, using submachine guns and 9 mm semi-automatic pistols. We were instructed to fire at the head with two quick shots, known as the double tap. 'The only difference between a good shot and a bad shot is five thousand rounds,' commented one of the SAS troopers and it made absolute sense to me.

We conducted team navigation exercises to hone bushcraft, learned camouflage and how to move silently during the day and at night, ran through obstacle courses and spent time in the gas house (a house literally pumped full of tear gas). We would enter the house, remove our gas masks, say our name and registered number, replace the gas mask and leave. This was easier said than done; that shit makes you feel like your head is on fire. We then got up the next day and did it all over again.

We had a blast (apart from the gas house) and got paid to do it. On nights when there was no training, we drank in the Snake Pit. Peter Kidd and I excitedly planned the future full-time squad over beers. Our running joke was that he'd be promoted to sergeant before me because he was senior by nine numbers. In those days of promotion by seniority, that was a valid point.

As was the custom, at the end of the course we were hosted to a magnificent formal dinner in the Sergeants Mess. The Australian Defence Force is well versed in pomp and pageantry, as well as the art of war. Formal dress, silver service, a four-course meal, the finest wines, speeches, toasts and, then, the final ritual of the night, the ceremonial passing of port to be drunk in beautiful silver goblets.

There was one problem. Someone among the fifty pissed Emergency Squad cops decided the silver goblets would make an excellent receptacles for the Stone's Green Ginger Wine that, for some strange reason, was the drink of choice after big nights in the Mess. So, it came to pass that a number of silver port goblets went missing for the night. The Army took a dim view of the police custom of borrowing things. Consequently, after 1984 we were banished to six-man tents and lined up to eat in the Other Ranks Mess, a far cry from the service at the Sergeants Mess.

———

As we packed up to leave that 1984 training camp, I was called to see the boss. 'Banksy, Harry wants to see you in his tent.' As usual, when a boss wanted to see me I immediately thought of what I'd done recently that may have broken some rules, but for once my conscience was clear. Well, it was fairly clear. I was sure I'd gotten away with 'borrowing' a car and making a trip to Surfers Paradise with two of the SAS instructors a few nights before.

Harry was Inspector Harry Edwards, who had been a part-time member of the Emergency Squad for years and was now in charge of support areas including the Task Force, Dog Squad, Bomb Disposal, Emergency Squad and the Rescue Squad. I found him sitting on a chair in his tent with a senior sergeant.

'Keith, come in,' he said. I was ready with my excuse for leaving the camp with the SAS boys. 'I'll get straight to the point.' Here we go, I thought.

'I'm starting a full time Emergency Squad with a core of men as a beginning. It will expand quickly but I want the right people to kick it off. You interested?' Only Victoria had a full-time tactical unit with its Special Operations Group. New South Wales had a core team of Special Weapons and Operations, the rest being part-time members. The other states and territories were still all part time, just like us. Harry's news meant we would finally be on a par with New South Wales and ultimately the same as Victoria.

Was I interested? I would have done anything to be doing this full time. I tried to contain my eagerness but I'm sure I sounded like an excited little kid. 'You bet I am, Boss. What's involved?'

I would need to apply for a transfer to the Task Force, which was one of the areas under his command, when the positions there were advertised internally. Once I was stationed with the Task Force, I could be quickly deployed for Emergency Squad roles and not be limited by part-time availability because I was a detective.

The Task Force comprised twenty cops, at that time all men, although there had been a policewoman in the team a few years before. It was classified as a uniform station and worked out of the second floor of the Police Depot in Petrie Terrace, right above Mobile Patrols. While it was officially a uniformed station, the only time Task Force members wore uniforms was to attend court cases.

The mission of the Task Force was simple: it was sent to areas known for 'hooliganism', where people were being bashed or harassed, to enforce street offences such as obscene language, indecent behaviour, disorderly behaviour and the like. Its members wore casual clothes and worked mainly afternoon shifts. Arrests were often violent and regularly resulted in the complementary charges of resisting arrest and assaulting police. The old rule every cop knew was: 'If you lay your hands on someone, you need to charge them with either resist or assault, preferably both.' And the laying on of hands wasn't in the biblical sense, more the Muhammad Ali sense.

The Taskies, as they were known, had a reputation for fixing problems, and probably causing some as well, but that's the way it was in the 1980s. Brisbane was a rough place, and the prevailing attitude was you don't send nice people to deal with thugs. My close mates Ando and Giblet, both of whom had been undercover in the Drug Squad with me, had gone to the Task Force and were loving the job.

Ando called it Mobile Patrols on steroids. He was a baby-faced guy a few months older than me, slightly built but as tough as nails. He'd been undercover when I'd just started, and he'd taught me a lot about how to act in that world. He looked even less like a cop than I did, if that was possible, and he loved the Task Force. 'Seriously, KJ,' he said when I asked him how it was, 'this is a great place to work. Heaps of overtime, wear whatever you want, get to belt pricks who deserve it and have a beer if you feel like it. They're all good blokes too.' Simple as that.

I understood that this offer meant I'd have to leave the CIB and officially go back to a uniformed position. Harry had been a detective and he knew what he was asking me to give up. 'If you come on board, you'll be one of the senior men in the permanent Emergency Squad when it starts. Before then though you'll be sent on courses interstate, starting with the bomb course in Bandiana, then you'll do the SAS course in Western Australia. I've already spoken to Peter Kidd and he'll be transferred to the squad as the first full timer and I'll get you on board as a full-time operator as quickly as I can. You don't have to give me an answer today, but I'd really like you to think about it. It won't happen for another nine or ten months, but I want to make sure I've got the right crew ready to go.'

I left with my head spinning. Here was a chance to do what I loved, but I needed to think about Harry's offer for a while. I enjoyed criminal investigation work, but I wanted to be a full-time tactical operator more. I'd achieved my detective designation and was getting bored. Maybe it *was* time for a move.

Within days, my mind was made up. Moving to the Task Force was my pathway to being part of the first permanent tactical team in Queensland.

A few months later, with an eye to the future, I applied for the Task Force vacancy when it was advertised in the *Police Gazette*.

TEN FOR YOU, TEN FOR US

My application for transfer was approved. After almost two years at Taringa CIB, I was one step closer to my dream of a full-time tactical weapons position. Peter Kidd had already started and was working as a bomb technician and Emergency Squad equipment officer. Needless to say, he was loving it.

One of the last jobs I was part of before my transfer from Taringa was a double kidnapping. More accurately, the same person was kidnapped twice.

Sharon was twenty-two, a student nurse who lived at home with her parents in Kenmore, a beautiful leafy suburb in our division. She was a nice young woman who'd been in an on-again, off-again relationship with a young man named David. Unfortunately, David was neither a student nor nice. He'd come to Brisbane from Sydney and by the age of twenty-five already had a record of offences to his name, ranging from assault to car theft. He'd spent his criminal apprenticeship in the notorious inner Sydney suburb of Darlinghurst, right beside the equally notorious Kings Cross. Perhaps Sharon saw something in David that others didn't. It's a never-ending story: good girl goes for bad boy hoping to change him.

In this case he didn't change, and Sharon finally broke off their relationship, tired of David's controlling personality, his fits of jealous rage and the seething violence. David didn't accept her decision. One evening, he grabbed her off the street and threw her into his Transit van. A witness to the abduction called police.

Even though my transfer was imminent, I was still an integral part of the response and worked with the team to track down the Transit before Sharon ended up badly injured or worse. Our inquiries with the Sydney CIB revealed David had some interesting associates, one of whom was the violent criminal Robert Rakich, well known as an enforcer in the Sydney underworld. He'd also been a self-appointed mentor for David, and this only increased our concern for Sharon's safety. We were concerned her body might end up in a shallow grave.

Police work is unpredictable. Civilians are fed a diet of television and film police dramas where hard-working detectives solve crimes through brilliant powers of observation and deduction. The reality is far different. There can be many lines of inquiry, each of which must be followed. Statements are taken and witnesses interviewed. In those days before the internet, we had to painstakingly read through hard copy criminal histories and intelligence reports to try to find patterns and likely scenarios. Investigations could go on for months, and in some cases years.

Sometimes, however, the universe gives you a lucky break. A New South Wales Highway Patrol cop had paid attention during his local morning briefing and had written down the details from the interstate BOLF (Be on the Lookout For) bulletin about the kidnapping. He was near Lennox Head on the Pacific Highway when he spotted a white Transit van with two occupants: one male, one female. He checked the number plate against his notes. Bingo.

Expecting a ticket, David pulled over in response to the lights and siren and found himself looking down the barrel of a Smith and Wesson police issue revolver. That's how Sharon was found, just bloody good police work. Seeing the joy on her parents' faces was wonderful. Of course, that night we celebrated with beers.

———

I moved on my transfer soon after and was back at the Police Depot in Petrie Terrace in my new job. The Task Force crew made me feel welcome and, as was the custom, I supplied a carton of beer on my first shift. We didn't get any work done that night. I was to learn that some nights were for work, some nights were for drinks.

The following morning I was nursing a slight hangover when Steve walked into the unit we shared. 'Hey, mate,' he said, 'remember Sharon, the girl from Kenmore?'

'Sure', I replied.

'You wouldn't believe it, he's grabbed her again.' David's lawyer had secured him bail and he'd obviously decided that the course of true love never did run smoothly, so another abduction was clearly the way to win her affections.

Steve and Dan (Denis Horne's regular partner) were running the job and alerted all police stations in Queensland and New South Wales. They had also contacted the Kings Cross CIB again, given Rakich's friendship with David.

This time David had succeeded in getting Sharon to Sydney's Kings Cross. Sharon managed to get away from David a few days later and found a phone to ring her parents. She was taken to safety and the hunt for David was on. He was found within the week and Dan and Steve flew to Sydney to interview him and extradite him back to Brisbane.

A week or so later, Steve and I were sitting on the balcony having a beer when he brought me up to date on what happened.

'So, we've got him in an interview room at Darlinghurst CIB. We're having a chat before the interview and he drops the story that he'd been found first by a couple of blokes from the Consorting Squad. They looked in his wallet, took the six hundred bucks he had, and let him go. They are fucking red hot down there.'

'No surprises there, mate,' I said. 'Is he back in custody?'

Steve nodded. 'And this time no bail. But Dan has to go back down and bring back Rakich. He was harbouring this prick.'

A couple of days later I was at Larry and Kathleen's unit in Auchenflower. Their tenth floor unit had views to the city and along the reach of the Brisbane River towards St Lucia. Kathleen and I had been in a relationship for a couple of months and I often spent the night there if I was on a late shift the following day. Larry was out of town on a job. As she was dressing for work the security intercom buzzed. I heard her answer. 'There are a couple of detectives from the Drug Squad who want to see you,' she said as she came into the bedroom, 'so I buzzed them in.' I hadn't told her about any of the uneasy conversations I'd had or the things I'd seen while I worked in the Drug Squad. I was immediately on my guard.

I answered the friendly knock at the door and opened it. Two men stood there with smiles on their faces. I recognised both. One of them, who I'll call Neil, had been part of a small cohort who had approached Larry and me in the Police Club a couple of years earlier with an offer to sell seized heroin and split the profits. We refused, and he hadn't spoken to me since that night. I breathed an internal sigh of relief when I saw the other detective. He was a nice bloke with a clean reputation.

'Come in, boys,' I said. 'How's things?' It was best to play it straight and pretend the heroin conversation had never happened.

Neil looked around. 'Someone else here?' he inquired when he heard Kathleen's hairdryer from the bathroom.

I shrugged. 'Only my girlfriend. Larry's away. What's up?'

Neil looked at me and smiled, but his eyes were cold and calculating. 'Just wanted to talk to you about something confidential.'

'Sure, come outside,' I said, keeping my face neutral. I led them out onto the large balcony and slid the door closed behind us. They both stood with their backs to the river and leant against the railing. Neil spoke. 'We hear a couple of the crew from Taringa are going to Sydney to extradite a bloke named Rakich.'

I nodded, now hyper vigilant. 'That's what I hear too.'

Neil looked steadily at me. 'It's worth ten grand if they don't bring him back.'

I was stunned. 'What?' I'm sure he mistook my shock for disbelief at the amount offered.

I looked at the other detective, the one I'd always thought was clean. He grinned. 'Yes, mate. Ten for you and ten for us. It's fair dinkum. The boys in Darlinghurst CIB have verified he's good for the cash.'

I knew this was dangerous ground. There were many stories of police being victimised for not going along with corrupt offers. There were rumours that others had been set up with stolen property or drugs. I knew police who'd been transferred to the country overnight as punishment. These two were senior to me and they would be believed over me if I reported what had just happened.

I pretended to consider the offer. I hoped my acting was as good as it had been when I was undercover. 'They're a pretty straight crew, boys,' I replied. 'Bob Dallow would go off his head if I even mentioned it.' Bob had a reputation as a hard man and tough cop, but a fiercely honest one.

'Fucking Dallow,' Neil cursed. 'Prick should be a priest. See what you can do. It's good money.' I saw them out and closed the door. Bob Dallow had nothing to do with the job on Rakich, but I knew Neil and his mate wouldn't push it if they thought Bob was involved. I decided the best course of action was to tell no one. I didn't want to have any of my mates at Taringa CIB tarnished in any way.

'They didn't want a coffee?' Kathleen asked as she left for work.

'Those bastards just offered me a bribe.'

She looked at me. 'Well, they're never setting foot in here again. How dare they do this in my house.' I couldn't help but smile. She was blonde, petite and gorgeous but had a spine of steel.

It was only later that I wondered how they knew I was there.

I was pissed off that they thought I was open to a bribe. I'd always made it clear that I wasn't bent and yet here they were. It became clear to me that they were so greedy they thought they'd make the approach anyway.

I recalled a day when I was still in the Drug Squad and was part of a team executing a search warrant on a typical Queensland weatherboard house in Everton Park, a suburb on Brisbane's north side. There were six or seven of us and the target was a major heroin dealer. I remember thinking it was strange that one of the higher ranked detectives was on the raid with us. They normally didn't leave the office unless there was an overnight trip or guaranteed overtime involved.

We arrived, one crew to the front and one to the back. The front crew kicked in the door and found the target inside. He was home alone and was detained. Then the team found a shoebox in a built-in wardrobe and opened it. It was stacked full of neat bundles of cash, each secured with a rubber band.

The search continued. I was under the house with another young detective named Roy going through boxes and containers for signs of drugs or other evidence when I heard the rear stairs creak and looked up to see the higher ranked detective coming towards us.

'Listen, boys, we're going to rip this cunt off,' he said. 'There's about a hundred and forty grand in that shoebox and plenty to go around. Just keep looking down here, you never know what else he's got.' With that, he turned on his heel and walked back up the stairs.

I looked at Roy and saw his eyes widen. I whispered, 'I'm not comfortable with this.'

He nodded. 'Me neither. This is just fucking wrong. What are we going to do?'

'I don't know, mate, let's just tell them they can have ours. Fuck, I don't like this at all.'

Thank god, we didn't need to have that conversation. The shoebox full of cash had been left with Alex, one of the more senior detectives and an honest man.

When the senior police officer came back downstairs he was livid, his face flushed with anger. 'Job's off. That fucking idiot Alex has laid the money out and taken photographs of it. There's no fucking way we can take it now.'

Roy and I made no comment. I whispered to Roy, 'Thank fuck.' He nodded.

But right now I needed a plan to protect myself. How many more of these bastards were bent? Queensland of the 1980s was a different world. Today one of the best resourced units in any police service is Ethical Standards, aggressively investigating any hint of corruption. In the 1980s it was best to shut up and get on with it. By going to Internal Investigations you were putting your own neck on the line. You didn't know who they knew or who they were protecting.

A few years earlier during an undercover job Larry and I had been introduced to a man referred to as 'Joe from Griffith'. He had named three very senior police as his friends and told us he was happy to do business even if we were cops, just like he did with his police friends, but he would kill us if he discovered we were undercover cops and we betrayed him. We recorded the meeting covertly and took a copy of the tape to Inspector Terry Channels of the Drug Squad, who told us he couldn't guarantee our safety if the undercover operation continued because the tape had already gone 'upstairs', code for the Commissioner. Here was an experienced and honest officer who knew about the presence of corruption at the highest levels in the Queensland Police Force, but he hadn't wanted to risk his career or his reputation, and our well-being, to take it further. I learned then, even as a constable, that it was not wise to trust too many people.

A week or so after the visit from Neil and his mate, I received a call at work from Neil asking if I'd had a chance to think about the Rakich offer. All I could think to say was that I couldn't do it because Bob and his crew wouldn't go for it. 'Yeah, I thought so, they're a bunch of fucking choirboys. They'd never make it in a real squad.' With that he hung up.

I didn't tell Steve about the attempted bribe. It was better he didn't know. As it turned out, Rakich refused to fly back to Queensland with Dan. Steve and another Emergency Squad member were instructed to drive to Sydney in a police van to bring Rakich back. Miraculously, Rakich was cured of his fear of flying once he saw the van and he flew back to Queensland with Dan.

Rakich was granted bail and promptly broke bail conditions and returned to Kings Cross. A few weeks later he was killed when a Ferrari he was a passenger in smashed into a concrete wall in Kings Cross. Maybe there is a divine plan for the universe after all.

When the Fitzgerald Inquiry into Queensland police was established a few years later, Neil resigned. Apparently, he 'had a better job'. The other officer who visited me that day in Brisbane stayed on. He retired years later as a very senior officer and collected his healthy superannuation payout. There were no consequences.

A few months after the bribe offer from Neil, Ando and I were having a beer with a couple of mates at the Police Club. A senior sergeant who was well known to be bent strolled over. 'Hello, Keith,' he said. 'Just thought I'd mention to you a friend of mine wanted me to have a chat.'

'Sure, what's up?' I replied.

'He lives over the border and apparently you met him a while ago. You've told a couple of blokes about a tape.' He was talking about 'Joe from Griffith' and by extension the senior police Joe had named. It didn't surprise me that this was coming from him. In fact, I was amazed it had taken so long for someone to raise it.

By now I'd had enough of this bullshit. It was time I sent a clear message that I wasn't one of them. 'That's right, I have. You let him and anyone else who's interested know that it's in a very safe place. In fact, there's more than one copy. But I'm sure there's no need for it to be played, I just like having it'. I knew I'd just made an enemy, but I was sick of this.

He looked back at me and nodded. 'I'll pass it on,' he said, smiling. 'Enjoy your beer.'

Ando looked at him as he walked away. 'Careful of that bastard, KJ,' Ando said as he watched the sergeant walk away. 'He's one of Murphy's mates.' I knew he was referring to the notorious Tony Murphy.

I've often wondered about the timing. Why would that senior sergeant have approached me then? I doubt it was a coincidence. He was well known to be right in the thick of the corrupt group of very senior police and was on first name terms with the Commissioner.

Queensland police history is littered with unsolved cases and many of them have the taint of corruption attached. Shirley Brifman was a high-class prostitute and brothel madam who had serviced a few senior police and paid off those same police to allow her to keep operating. She was to be the star witness in the corruption trial of senior Queensland detective Tony Murphy when she died in mysterious circumstances in a police safe house in 1972. On the advice of police that there were 'no suspicious circumstances' the coroner ruled the death as suicide. After Brifman's death, the case against Murphy collapsed and he went on to become an Assistant Commissioner. Perhaps he was just lucky or perhaps he was looked after by his mates. Either way, he was a dangerous and corrupt man.

I was in this job for life and these bastards weren't going to change that. I just needed to keep my head above water and not fall into the abyss with them. By moving to the Task Force I would no longer have to deal with those few corrupt cops who had so much influence.

THE TASK FORCE

In the 1960s every police force in Australia had a squad whose job it was to deal with the youth gangs who roamed the streets engaging in petty crime and bashing anyone who crossed their paths. Anyone who grew up in that period could name the gangs on the streets in their city. They were different from state to state, but the police response was identical: find the leaders, give them a flogging and lock up everyone else.

This approach is unheard of in modern policing, but it was effective in its own way. Perhaps inspired by those times, the Metropolitan Task Force was formed in the mid-1970s to deal with the increasing street violence across Brisbane. I saw and experienced that violence as a young uniform cop walking the beat in the city. Most afternoon shifts guaranteed there'd be someone out to punch a cop in the face just for the fun of it.

The Task Force consisted of twenty cops, mostly senior constable rank with three sergeants and one senior sergeant all working in casual clothes, who were part of the support services area commanded by Harry Edwards. My old undercover mates Ando and Giblet were in the Taskies already, while Don, Geoff and Dennis were members of the Emergency Squad. Our remit was anywhere that anti-social activity threatened the peaceful pursuits of citizens.

In other words, places where pissed young men were likely to play up and want to fight. We worked at the cricket, football, rock concerts and any other places that may have had a problem with public order, as well as pubs with a reputation for violence.

The easiest way to deal with bad behaviour was to enforce the Vagrants, Gaming and Other Offences Act provisions for public behaviour. As strange as it probably sounds in this era, anyone using the words *fuck* or *cunt* in a public place could be arrested for the use of obscene language. They'd often swing a punch at your head or would try to pull away from your grasp. The first action resulted in a charge of assaulting police, the second in a charge of resisting arrest. When someone was arrested and charged on all three accounts—obscene language, assault police and resist arrest—that was known as the Ham, Cheese and Tomato or the Hamburger with the Lot. Once the police van was full of miscreants, they were taken to the watchhouse, formally charged and given the choice of paying a fine of ten dollars per charge and not having to appear in court or pleading not guilty.

In those days, telling a cop to get fucked would find you in the watchhouse standing in front of the charge counter reassessing your actions. It may seem excessive by today's standards, but it provided an immediate consequence for being a smart arse. It also cleaned up a lot of problems.

Some arrests were more pleasing than others, such as the day Ando and I were at the Gabba on duty watching the crowd at a one-day cricket match. It wasn't unusual for groups of blokes at the cricket to drink as much as they could, and for the combination of beer and testosterone to kick in sometime in the afternoon.

Ando was sitting beside me. We were in our work attire, T-shirts, shorts, runners and baseball caps, and looked like just another couple of blokes in the crowd. Some uniformed police, including a particularly beautiful policewoman nicknamed Sam, walked past the stand of seats we were in. Protected by the anonymity of the crowd, the hero sitting beside us yelled, 'I'd like to fuck the cop.' Within seconds he was on his way to a Ham, Cheese and Tomato as Ando and I dragged him away. I was willing to bet he'd be careful about declaring his romantic feelings in public for a while after that. (Ironically, if Sam had got hold of him, he would have been far worse off. She was certainly gorgeous, but she was also more than capable of dishing out a belting to anyone who needed it.)

But the Task Force wasn't all about arresting loudmouths at the cricket. We often had to get down and dirty. It requires a lot of force to restrain a person who doesn't want to be held down and it often involves two or three people grappling and rolling around in the grime of a footpath or car park. There were no tasers, capsicum spray or extendable batons in those days, so you just learned to fight with what you had. I worked out quickly to wear clothes I didn't mind getting torn or ruined.

The Task Force went hands on with all kinds of society. We even had an annual event where we engaged in philosophical differences with an outlaw motorcycle gang. Every year the Task Force would be rostered for duty at The Ekka—the Royal Brisbane Show—which was one of the city's main attractions for the year. The Woodchop Bar was a favourite venue for people who liked a beer while watching the woodchopping competition in the arena. It was also the preferred location for patched members of the Black Uhlans outlaw motorcycle gang to congregate and by extension the preferred location for the Task Force. At my first Ekka, Ando told me the rules. 'Mate, they think they're tough in numbers and they like to throw their weight around with people trying to have a quiet beer. We just mingle and wait. As soon as they start their shit, we start ours.' Within the hour, we were going toe to toe with the Black Uhlans. They lost.

I enjoyed the Task Force more than I thought I would. It was back-to-basics policing and with a great team of men. We didn't just arrest for street offences; we responded to urgent jobs that came up when we were on the road and, importantly, we could immediately react to siege or armed offender situations in our capacity as Emergency Squad members. All in all, it was a great time and place to be a cop.

COX THE FOX

Wednesday 30 October 1985 was a typical Brisbane spring day. The sky was a beautiful clear blue and the temperature hovered around 21 degrees. People in their summer clothes were happily going about their lives.

I, too, was happily going about my day sitting in a cramped VW surveillance van with four other cops. Like me, three of them were Emergency Squad operators dressed in black overalls with bullet resistant vests underneath. We were armed with handguns and Heckler and Koch (H&K) submachine guns. The other occupant was wearing jeans, a T-shirt and a three-day growth. He was sitting in the front passenger seat idly looking out the window. Often, when people see news footage of tactical police, it's the exciting part, abseiling out of helicopters or smashing in doors. What they don't know about is the mind-numbing boredom of sitting in one place for hours trying to stay focused and not being able to move apart from wriggling your toes in your boots to keep the blood flowing. But then, you are expected to be able to launch straight into action. It doesn't matter how physically fit you are, this is never an easy thing to do. Snipers have it worse: once they have secreted themselves in a hide to watch a stronghold they can sometimes be there for a day or more.

On this day, our operation was relatively short as far as time in the van went. We'd been in place since 6 am and it was now approaching 8.55 am. 'Fourth week in a row, I wish these blokes would fucking get on with it,' muttered Geoff, one of the other Emergency Squad members. None of us replied. It looked like it would be another quiet day just as the previous three Wednesdays had been. I looked down at my H&K 9-mm submachine gun and, out of habit, checked to make sure the thirty-round magazine was seated firmly home. I was already thinking of what I was going to do for the rest of the shift.

Our van was nestled among cars in the car park of the Mayne Junction railway yards in Bowen Hills, which was the site of the Queensland Railways head office. We'd been there the previous three Wednesdays for the 9.30 am weekly cash payroll delivery in an armoured van. A Brisbane detective had received information that this payroll was in the sights of one of the most notorious armed robbers in Australia, Melville Peter Schnitzerling, also known as Russell 'Mad Dog' Cox.

Cox had a long history of violence. He had escaped from the 'escape proof' Katingal security unit of Sydney's Long Bay gaol in 1977, where he had been serving a life sentence. Cox was without doubt a violent man but, unlike most armed robbers, he was also intelligent and resourceful. He was a fitness fanatic, non-smoker and non-drinker with a love of running and yoga. Cox also knew the tricks of counter-surveillance and was adept with weapons. In short, he was a professional in a field where many others tried to emulate him but no one came close. He was violent and calculated, certainly not mad. He was also an expert in disguise and could change his appearance quickly. His nickname should have been Cox the Fox.

The plan had been for the guards in the armoured van to emerge from the rear of the van with the cash sacks in hand. When the robbers challenged the guards and had taken the bags, we were to emerge from our surveillance van and order them to drop their weapons and get on the ground. The rules of engagement were clear: if the robbers presented a threat to anyone's life, either ours or someone else's, we were to fire. These rules applied to every police action, but in our case they were always included in our briefings.

I'd been a member of the squad for almost three years and had been in numerous hot entries to buildings, but this was the first job where I'd sat in wait for an armed robbery. We were keen for the payroll to arrive so we could get back to the office and out of our blacks into more comfortable clothes for the rest of the shift. Complacency, however, can get you killed. I was about to learn an important lesson.

The radio crackled. 'There's a cream Valiant sedan that's driven through a couple of times,' one of the surveillance team reported. 'Driver doesn't look like the target but would be worth checking it out.'

I looked at Jonah, our team leader. 'What do you think?' I asked.

He replied, 'Could be. Time to switch on, boys.'

The same voice came across the radio again. 'The Valiant's leaving towards Abbotsford Road. Anyone there to take it away?'

Detective Sergeant George Sharry and Detective Senior Constable Kim Roylance were parked in a side street. They were dressed in business clothes and were driving an unmarked CIB car. They were both from the Armed Hold Up Squad, but their role was not to be part of the 'takeout' team. Once Cox and any associates had been detained, George and Kim were the official arrest team.

That was the plan, anyway. But as any cop with operational experience will tell you, plans frequently don't go the way you'd like.

The Valiant left the railway yards and drove away, passing the street where Sharry and Roylance were parked. 'We can see it,' Roylance radioed to us. 'We'll have a talk with the driver.'

Neither Sharry nor Roylance were armed. Their firearms were, in fact, in a briefcase on the back seat of their car. 'We didn't need to have our guns, we were only there to be the arrest team after the Emergency Squad had taken the crooks out,' Roylance said later. 'There was no indication that the driver was anyone other than someone who'd driven through the car park.'

They followed the Valiant sedan along Abbottsford Road, activating the siren and waving for the driver to pull over. The Valiant drove into a dead-end street near a car rental yard and stopped. Sharry got out of the car and walked towards the Valiant as the driver opened his door and walked towards the detectives.

It was 9.00 am and traffic was busily making its way along Abbotsford Road. Sporting a mullet and moustache and wearing jeans and a white singlet under an unbuttoned red and white checked flannelette shirt, the Valiant driver seemed affable enough as he walked towards the police car.

'G'day, mate,' Sharry announced as he approached the driver. 'Police.'

Looking steadily at Sharry, the man produced a revolver from his waistband under the shirt. It was Cox. 'Get on the fucking ground,' he snarled.

Roylance, who was still on the passenger side of the car, ducked down behind the door for cover.

Sharry was now prone on the ground with Cox's gun pointed at his head. 'Get out here or I'll shoot your mate,' Cox demanded of Roylance.

Roylance walked around and lay on the ground beside Sharry.

Cox was as cool as a cucumber. He stood over them. 'One murmur, one move, and I'll shoot both you bastards dead,' he said.

Cox then moved to the police car, removed the keys from the ignition, picked up the briefcase and locked the doors. He calmly walked back to the Valiant and drove away.

Because Cox had locked the police car, Sharry and Roylance couldn't use the radio. They had to run into the car rental yard to use the phone to call Police Operations for backup.

Back in the van, I said to Jonah, 'Do you think we should go and back up the stick ups [the name most of us used to refer to the Armed Hold Up squad]?'

'No, our job is to protect the money,' he said just as the call came in from Police Operations to assist detectives on Abbotsford Road in trouble with a gunman. We were on the site within minutes.

Sharry was succinct. 'It was fucking Cox and the cunt stole our guns. That way,' he said, pointing in the direction Cox had fled.

We drove off at speed, but he was gone.

The Valiant was found hours later in an industrial car park in Alderley with a tarpaulin thrown over the top. A search of the car found the stolen briefcase with its contents intact, including the police revolvers. There were also personal papers with a Noosa address.

We travelled to Noosa and raided that address, but the trail was cold. I didn't know it then, but this wasn't the last time Cox would be in our sights.

What did give me chills was the .308 calibre Heckler and Koch assault rifle with a loaded thirty-round magazine that Cox had left behind in the Valiant's boot. He had clearly intended to use this in the armoured van robbery. This was a man who didn't fuck around. Our weapons would have been insignificant in a gunfight against that rifle.

I was never complacent again.

OPERATION BOREHEAD

The four men living rough in two campsites amid mulga scrub were oblivious to the RAAF F-111 fighter jet thousands of feet above. They were going about their daily routine of ensuring the crop was flourishing. The country around Boatman, near Charleville in western Queensland and over seven hundred kilometres from Brisbane, had proven to be ideal for the hundreds of almost mature cannabis plants. The crop was accessible only by four-wheel drive along rough bush tracks. Unless you came by air.

A few days after the F-111 had returned to the Royal Australian Air Force base at Amberley, Inspector Harry Edwards held a briefing in his office for a job code-named Operation Borehead. 'The RAAF have picked up what appears to be a substantial crop near Charleville. They were doing a routine fly-over taking high speed photos of the ground as part of a training exercise and when the photos were developed, they found this and passed it to the Drug Squad.' He handed around a set of black and white photos that showed a large crop of around two hectares. 'The Drug Squad have information that this crop is linked to the mafia in Griffith. They want to raid it and our job is to go in first and secure the targets.'

Griffith again! I wondered whether Joe was part of this. 'I'm sure you'll all be happy to know we won't be driving in, we'll be using 9 Squadron helicopters,' Harry announced. The Emergency Squad had worked with 9 Squadron as part of counter terrorist training in the lead up to the 1982 Commonwealth Games, but this time it would be the real thing. I could feel the excitement in the briefing room. Peter Kidd caught my eye and grinned. This job was just getting better and better.

RAAF's 9 Squadron has a significant place in the history of the Australian Defence Force. The squadron had been deployed to Vietnam as a fighting unit and crews were regularly exposed to ground fire, night operations including evacuation of wounded soldiers and landing patrols into hot fire zones. During the battle of Long Tan in 1966 two 9 Squadron helicopters flew under appalling weather conditions and heavy enemy fire to resupply 6 RAR's D Company, which was outnumbered and low on ammunition. Later, in 1969, four of the squadron's helicopters were armed with forward firing miniguns and rocket pods on each side. Pilots who had flown combat missions in Vietnam were still flying with 9 Squadron and I felt very comfortable knowing they'd be taking us in.

The briefing continued in detail. We were to be divided into four teams. I would be the team leader of one; Peter Kidd the team leader of another. There were two identified target locations, and both looked like rough sheds. The RAAF photographs showed vehicles and movement at one of the target sites near a dam. Three assault teams would land and secure that site and my team would land and secure the other. The targets were about five hundred metres apart.

My team's target location was regarded as a secondary site only and the planning assumed it to be unoccupied. I was disappointed but not totally surprised. Steve and I had been chastised by the squad senior sergeant for being too jovial during a recent job when we had tried to lighten the mood by telling a couple of jokes while sitting in the back of a Toyota troop carrier for a few hours. It was the senior sergeant's style to punish any transgression by giving you a shit job the next chance he got. Steve, as usual, was my number two and I had Geoff and Bergs, two other Task Force cops, making up the remainder of my assault team.

The next two days were spent preparing equipment and planning for various scenarios. The four assault teams would each fly in Iroquois helicopters from Amberley Air Base in the afternoon and spend the night at a staging area about thirty minutes flight from the crop location. We would fly to the targets just on dawn the following day. Harry and two sergeants would be flying in a Chinook helicopter, an ugly tandem rotor machine primarily used for troop and artillery transport and heavy machinery lifting. Another Chinook would transport equipment required by the RAAF crews.

To say I was excited to be on this job was an understatement. Never in my wildest dreams had I imagined I would be part of a tactical helicopter assault on a major mafia-backed cannabis crop. Of course, we played it cool and pretended not to be excited, but I knew we were all eager to get on with one of the biggest jobs we'd ever done.

A couple of days later we travelled to the Amberley Air base in Toyota troop carriers and unmarked cars. The weather was starting to turn bad and rain was falling, not heavily but enough to be annoying. I hoped it wouldn't ground the aircraft.

The safety briefing was conducted by RAAF officers and the flight crews were announced. Each Iroquois would have a pilot, co-pilot and crew chief. Our pilot, Kevin, was a Vietnam veteran and immediately made us feel confident that we were in the right hands. His colleagues were around our age and seemed to be just as excited as we were.

We walked to our helicopter, strapped on our harnesses and donned headsets to allow communication with the RAAF crew. I couldn't wipe the smile off my face, I loved helicopters. As we lifted off, however, my excitement quickly disappeared as Kevin's voice crackled through my headset. 'Okay, men, we're flying into a serious storm and we'll be operating on instruments only. Zero visibility. Make sure you keep your harnesses tight; it might get a bit bumpy.'

Within ten minutes we could see nothing through the windshield because of the driving rain. The Great Dividing Range was somewhere ahead. I was now terrified. I concentrated on my breathing and as I listened to Kevin and his co-pilot calmly going through instrument readings, I looked over at the crew chief. He was asleep.

The crew flew by instruments for almost an hour when suddenly the sky cleared and the night sky was ablaze with stars. We were well away from the light pollution of the city. An hour later we landed in a clear area in the middle of the mulga scrub. We got out, secured our gear and put our sleeping bags in one of the two Chinooks. The Chinook crews produced portable gas barbeques and we were treated to a steak dinner. No sleeping on the ground and eating cold cans of baked beans for us.

I slept fitfully that night, not because I was uncomfortable but because I couldn't wait for the morning. We were up at 4.00 am, and after tea and coffee we double checked our kit, actioned our weapons and climbed aboard our assigned helicopters. Steve was sitting beside me, and Geoff and Bergs were behind us. I turned to them. 'Okay, boys, be careful and watch each other's backs. Good luck.' They all gave me a thumbs up as the turbines whirred and the unmistakable *wop wop* of the rotors became louder. Within minutes we were in the air and on our way.

There is no bigger buzz than being with your team at the sharp end of policing on your way to a high-risk target. It is adrenaline inducing, exciting and frightening. Fear is essential in the tactical world. It means you won't make stupid mistakes. I looked out of the open door and saw the other three Iroquois flying in combat formation. I felt Steve's hand on my shoulder and looked over to him. He motioned for me to sit back and pointed to a small camera he had in his hand. The senior sergeant had expressly directed in the briefing, 'No cameras are to be taken, this is not a holiday. If anyone does take a camera there'll be disciplinary action.' Rules are only rough guides to real life, and it would have been a shame not to have some mementos of this raid. I knew we'd get in the shit for it at some point, but I'd worry about that when it happened.

Twenty or so minutes later, the pilot's voice came clearly through the headphones. 'Ten minutes to target.' I replied, 'Roger,' and turned to the team, relaying the message to them via hand signals. We all checked our magazines to ensure they were seated home in our weapons, double checked safety and started to switch on mentally. The rush that I was continually chasing was again coursing through my body. Adrenaline was now my drug of choice.

Even though we had been told our target location was expected to be unattended, we were still ready. Just in case.

Our pilot's voice, 'One minute.'

As we banked over the target, I saw a tin shed with what seemed like hectares of cannabis plants perfectly planted in rows nearby. We dropped toward the target at high speed. 'This was what it was like in Vietnam?' the co-pilot asked.

'Yep, the only things missing are the rockets and miniguns,' the pilot replied calmly as he expertly slowed the chopper and angled in between the trees to hover about a metre above the ground, allowing us to jump out. It had rained overnight, and the ground was wet and muddy. Within seconds of us hitting the ground, the Iroquois was gone. It hovered above to relay communications to the command Chinook with Harry Edwards and the sergeants on board.

I exited on the left side of the chopper with Bergs, and Steve and Geoff had jumped from the right. We were moving with weapons up and focused on what we thought was an empty shed when suddenly a man burst out of the entrance and ran away from us.

The four men had been asleep when we landed. They'd spent the previous day checking the watering systems were working properly and verifying the booby traps they'd set were still secure. The traps weren't sophisticated, just fishing lines with sharpened fishhooks wrapped around plants and a few holes with sharpened sticks, but they were better than nothing. They knew the chances of police walking into the crop were low and that they'd hear a four-wheel drive from miles away, which would give them time to get ready for unwelcome guests. The shed had rifles and a pump action shotgun within easy reach, and to top it off the Doberman and German Shepherds that lived with them didn't like strangers either. They'd been living rough for months, but the crop was nearly ready and they were going to be paid enough not to have to work for quite a while.

I yelled, 'Bergs, with me,' and gave chase. I could see Steve and Geoff in my peripheral vision still moving towards the target location. Within seconds we were past the shed and running after the escaping man. Then I heard a burst of automatic fire from an M16 rifle, which I knew both Steve and Geoff were carrying. As the sound of the shots reverberated through the air, the man dropped to the ground and screamed, 'Don't shoot! I give up.' My first thought was that Steve or Geoff had shot someone and I was pissed off that I'd missed out on the action.

Bergs and I secured our target's hands behind his back with cable ties and walked him back to the shed. I looked up and saw the Chinook and our Iroquois hovering a couple of hundred feet above us. As we got closer, I spotted three men face down on the ground with their hands cable tied behind them, and Steve and Geoff standing nearby. 'What happened?' I asked.

'M16 one, Doberman nil,' Steve replied nonchalantly, pointing to the corner of the shed. The Doberman lay on the ground with bullet holes in its chest, its teeth bared in the rictus of death. Steve and Geoff had been moving closer to the target shed when the Doberman and a German Shepherd had burst from the open doorway and ran towards them at full speed in attack mode. Steve reacted instinctively and fired a three-round burst at the Doberman, stopping it in mid stride and killing it instantly. The other dog skidded to a halt, turned and ran away into the scrub never to be seen again. Which just goes to show German Shepherds are smarter than Dobermans.

The other three men had been inside and had come out on their knees with hands in the air at the sound of gunfire. The rifles and shotgun in the shed remained against the wall, untouched. Which just goes to show, some people are smarter than German Shepherds and Dobermans.

The other target site was empty, which left the three other teams disappointed. Plans have a habit of going sideways, and this was a good lesson for all of us. Assumptions have little place in high-risk operations.

It took the Drug Squad and other police about thirty minutes to arrive by road, giving us the opportunity to take some trophy pictures for posterity while Harry was distracted.

One of the poor bastards lying face down on the ground was wearing a Tooheys' branded shirt. 'Geez, I reckon I'll be having a Tooheys a long time before you do, mate,' Ando remarked. All the bloke could manage in response was, 'Yeah, well you can get fucked.'

The crop was spread over hectares and had been very well tended. Some of the plants were taller than we were, and the quality was excellent. Losing this would easily cost the Griffith mafia a couple of million dollars. We learned later that two of the mafia principals had been on the site two days earlier. That's how it went sometimes, just bad timing.

We were back on our helicopter and flying to the holding area where we had slept the night before within the hour. As we landed, the RAAF guys were happily cooking up a breakfast of bacon, eggs, sausages, tea, coffee and toast. Harry organised a Yippee shoot for them to say thank you. The RAAF guys were like little kids as they excitedly lined up to take their turn firing submachine guns, M16 rifles and shotguns for fun all the while still keeping safety considerations foremost in mind. We happened to have 3000 rounds with us and by the end of the Yippee that supply was totally exhausted.

After the Yippee, we opened a couple of eskies that had been stored beside the barbeques to reveal ice cold cans of beer. 'Got any Tooheys?' Ando inquired with a look of innocence. The RAAF sure knew how to travel.

We flew back to the Amberley base a few hours later and were promptly hosted to a long celebratory session in the Officers Mess by our RAAF friends. I don't remember getting home.

I woke the next morning with the absolute certainty that I wanted to do this job forever.

BROWN ROCKS

Larry was tired. Tired of dealers, tired of bullshitting to people and tired of not having a normal life. It seemed like decades since he'd been Larry the cop, since he'd been able to meet someone new and tell them what he did for a living. He was proud of being a cop, but now he was getting to the stage where he didn't know what was real anymore.

This time he was Jason, a heroin dealer looking to expand his supply chain. He was on his way to a buy, but first he had to make up for losing his temper on the phone to a woman he was relying on to arrange that buy.

He parked in front of the yard of a house in Sandgate. Lawn needs mowing, he thought as he walked up and knocked on the door. It slowly opened to reveal a young woman looking nervously at him. She was slim, in her mid-twenties with dyed blonde hair and the hollow eyes of a regular heroin user. 'Hi Jason,' she said nervously. 'Come in.'

Larry walked inside and turned to her. 'Hey, Shelly, sorry I went off this morning on the phone, but I hate wasting my day waiting for fucking dealers who promise and don't deliver.' He knew he couldn't back down, after all he was supposed to be a heroin dealer who had people to look after. He was a busy man. He regretted yelling at Shelly that morning and knew this whole job was getting to him. It wasn't her fault the dealer was late.

'I'm sorry, Jason,' she said looking at the floor, chewing her bottom lip.

'Don't worry about it. As long as he shows, it's cool.'

She looked up and smiled. 'Oh yeah, he's on his way right now. Thanks for being cool about it, I don't want to upset anybody.'

Larry had a twinge of conscience. When this operation was over she'd be charged with supply heroin because she'd set up the meeting with the dealer, and she was apologising for wasting his time. *Fuck, I'm starting to hate this job*, he thought. The moment passed and he was back in character. 'Okay, I hope he is. I've got people to see.'

With that, the back door opened and a man about Shelly's age walked in. 'Hi, I made it,' he said, smiling at Larry. 'Sorry you had to wait, but I had to wait around for the gear. You know how it is.'

Larry wanted to say, Y*es, I know how it is, this is the only business where no one expects anyone else to be on time.* Instead, he nodded. He'd met Gary a couple of days earlier through Shelly and this was the first buy from him. He knew Gary would be giving Shelly a hit of the smack in return for her introduction to a new customer, but he didn't know whether Gary used.

Gary reached into the shoulder bag he was carrying and produced a tab of silver foil. He looked pointedly at Shelly, who turned and left the room. He handed the tab to Larry. 'There you go, Jason.'

Larry opened the foil and saw brown rocks. Good shit, but you had to play hard to get. 'Not bad, bit small for a gram.'

Gary smiled at him. 'Mate, this gear is excellent. It's a good sixty to seventy per cent pure, so you've got to take it easy. You use?'

Larry shook his head. 'In it for the money, mate. My business partner doesn't want anyone who uses working for him. Strictly business.'

'That's smart. I had a habit for years, then I kicked it. But now this gear has come along it's so good I've started using again. You'll have to cut it down a lot, otherwise someone will OD, so make sure you do.'

'Is this the gear we were talking about when we met?' Larry asked.

'Sure is, my mate bought two pounds of it. Took him thirteen months to get it into the country. I've seen the bags; they've still got the original stamps on them.' If that was true, the heroin had come from the Golden Triangle.

Larry looked at his watch. 'Okay, mate. I've got someone else to meet. I'll take this to my partner, and we'll let you know. If it's as good as you say, I want to talk about an ounce. Cool?'

Gary smiled. 'There's plenty to go round, mate. Listen, I'll give you my number,' he said, handing Larry a piece of paper. 'Don't worry about calling Shelly anymore, she doesn't need to know what we do. Call me when you're ready.'

As Larry drove back to Brisbane, he kept an eye on the rear-view mirror, just as he had for the last five years.

I need a drink and a joint, he thought. *I also need to get out of this job.*

———

I caught up with Larry regularly. Kathleen and I were now a couple, so I spent a lot of time at the unit they shared with its beautiful views to the Brisbane River. The balcony was a favourite place for us to talk, or rather for me to listen when Larry needed someone to talk to. I was working regular shifts and had some routine in my life. For Larry it was the opposite. His undercover life consisted of doing what he needed to do when it needed to be done.

One afternoon we were sitting on the balcony when he said: 'I'm scoring brown rock smack from this guy and he arranges for me to meet his dealer in a pub car park. The analysis shows this gear is over seventy-five per cent pure even though he's stepped on it a couple of times,' meaning the dealer had added milk powder or similar to the heroin to increase the weight and therefore his profit margin. This happened all the way along the supply chain, from the importer to the street junkie. That was how overdoses happened. If a user developed a tolerance to heroin that was ten per cent pure, normal for street smack, and they scored something that was thirty per cent pure, it was lights out for good.

I drank my beer, knowing he had to talk about his undercover life to someone who understood. 'The main dealer comes to the car and he's with a little girl, about eight or nine. She's holding a small cardboard box about the size of a fucking tissue box. He lets go her hand and she walks over to where we're standing beside my car and hands the box to my guy. She says in this little-girl-wanting-to-please voice, "This is for you, Gary, from my daddy." There's five fucking grams of smack inside.'

I shook my head. 'So he's using his daughter for cover?'

I could see the sadness in Larry's eyes. 'They laugh about it and how the cops would never search a little girl. These bastards have no soul. KJ, I have to get out before I do something to them.'

I gripped his shoulder. What had once been an adventure was now destroying him.

BANDIANA

On 24 February 1986 I was at the gates of the Army base at Bandiana some four kilometres outside Wodonga in Victoria with Greg, another Emergency Squad member. From Townsville, he was a few years older and a former Army commando. Harry Edwards had been true to his word when he told me he would send me on training courses as part of my development and here I was on a bomb response course. Until then sections other than the Emergency Squad had taken on the role in Queensland, but as part of Harry's plan to justify the creation of a full-time squad, he'd successfully lobbied to have it taken on by us.

Funded by the federal government, the course was attended by two representatives from each state and territory police force, most of whom were from the scientific or forensic sections in their respective organisations. On the second day Jim Venn and Scowie, two Victorian Special Operations Group (SOG) members, arrived from Melbourne. They gravitated to us once they realised we were tactical operations cops and spoke the same language. The SOG had been formed as a full-time unit in 1977 and was the model for other police forces looking to do the same. Jim was over 190 centimetres tall and all muscle. He looked like he belonged on a recruiting poster and, in fact, some years later that's precisely what happened. Scowie was a shorter version of Jim. I quickly learned that the SOG required extreme levels of fitness to pass the selection process and to remain in the group. But for all their toughness and obvious abilities, they were two of the funniest men I'd met.

Over the next four weeks, we learned about the world of explosives and bomb disposal. Our instructors were a mix of Army explosive experts and police bomb disposal operators. This was a world I never imagined I'd be part of, and I soaked up everything I could.

Even though it was a lifetime ago, what we learned on the course is still highly sensitive and classified. I will only say that in order to learn how to dismantle improvised explosive devices, you need to know how to make them. On the second day we were taken to the firing range, where there was a line of cars obtained from wrecking yards. 'You have one of these each,' the chief instructor announced. 'Over the next four weeks, you will learn to set explosive charges and methodically blow these into little pieces.' And that's exactly what we did.

We were taught how to make improvised explosive devices and to use various means of detonation including tilt switches, collapsing electronic circuits and timer switches .We also made bombs of various makes and configurations. I was particularly interested to learn that the purpose of the bulky bomb suit that is often worn by bomb squad operators is not to protect them. It is designed to keep their body parts in one place if the bomb they're working on detonates. Good to know.

The police instructors were keen to teach us about hand entries, how to cut into suspected bombs and disarm them by cutting wires leading to the source of detonation to preserve evidence. The army instructors preferred to disrupt, or blow up, suspicious objects using a robot. When we were told the story of a leading bomb technician in the United States who'd been killed while he was attempting a hand entry on a pipe bomb, the Army instructors loved the acronym I created as a potential course motto: HELF, *Hand Entry, Like Fuck!* The police instructors were less appreciative.

HELF also found a place on one of the cars we'd been assigned to destroy. Originally spray painted with a version of the Looney Tunes Tassie Devil cartoon character Taz flipping the finger at the world, we took the bonnet off the car and gave it to a local spray painter in Wodonga. He painted on the course number and the names of the participants on each side of Taz with a large HELF at Taz's feet and the word POLICE above his head. That bonnet became our squad mascot and ended up being proudly displayed in the classroom for future courses.

True to form for every course held on a military base, we consumed alcohol every night of the four weeks in the Sergeants Mess. Official Australian Defence Force messes operated on a tax-free basis. That meant the average price of a large beer was forty cents. As one Northern Territory cop wryly observed, 'At that price, the more you drink the more money you save.' And if another excuse was needed to drink beer, the Army instructors told us that handling explosives increased blood pressure markedly and drinking beer reduced it. So, from a medical perspective, it made complete sense to partake.

It was in the mess over beers that I learned Jim Venn (Venny to his mates, a nickname that someone had put seconds of thought into) was already a veteran of two gun battles. In 1983, as a member of the Major Crime Squad, he and a colleague had intercepted a sedan containing an escaped prisoner and a hostage. The escapee made the error of raising a sawn-off shotgun and pointing it at

Venny, who promptly shot him in the head with his police shotgun. The thick windshield glass that Venny had fired two blasts into deflected the .32 calibre shotgun pellets enough not to kill the escapee, although he wouldn't feel well for quite some time.

Two years later Venny was in the SOG. He was part of an assault team executing a warrant in the Melbourne suburb of Wantirna to arrest neo-Nazi Tom Messenger. Messenger was armed with a pistol and a military M1 carbine rifle and opened fire on the SOG team as they entered a hallway inside the house. One of Messenger's shots hit Venny in the bullet-resistant vest he was wearing. As he dropped to his knee with the impact, another SOG officer returned fire and killed Messenger instantly. Neither Venny nor I knew then that our paths would continue to cross over the next decade and that he would be instrumental in the direction my life would later take.

When the course was over, I returned to Brisbane as a qualified bomb technician, another step forward in the full-time tactical operations goal I had set for myself. I was envious of the full-time SOG in Victoria, but I knew a group would be established in Queensland sooner or later. I was prepared to wait. My life was about being at the sharp end and I'd do whatever it took to stay there.

HALLEY'S COMET AND COX

The arrival of Halley's Comet in 1986 had excited astronomers and ordinary folk around the world for years beforehand and Australia would be one of the best places on the planet to see the spectacular comet. The 'long-haired star', last seen in 1910, had been considered a bad omen and been blamed for everything from the death of kings to natural disasters. It was described by an historian in AD 66 as a 'star resembling a sword' and was immortalised in the famous Bayeux Tapestry, depicting King Harold II and fearful soldiers watching it streak through the sky before his defeat at the Battle of Hastings in 1066. In 1986, we would experience some of the curse of the comet.

3.00 am, Friday 8 April 1986
'Fuck me, is that what the fuss is all about?' Steve asked as we looked up at the tiny smudge of light on the horizon of the black western Queensland sky. Our convoy had stopped beside the road to take a break during the long drive from Brisbane.

Fifteen of us had been activated from the Emergency Squad and our convoy of unmarked cars included the Dog Squad and detectives from the Armed Hold Up Squad. Our mission was to arrest Russell Cox, who was believed to be in a farmhouse a few hours further away. Detective Sergeant George Sharry was in charge of the detectives and he was still carrying a grudge against Cox after being held at gunpoint by him only months beforehand.

'Well, that's disappointing,' I replied to Steve. We'd both been looking forward to seeing the comet without the light pollution of Brisbane and expected it to be more spectacular than this tiny fuzzball. This was supposed to be the best time and the best place in the world to view it.

'Yep, pretty underwhelming,' George said behind us. 'Boys, we need to talk about the job,' he continued. 'Come with me for a minute. I want to show you something.'

We walked over to his unmarked car. He opened the boot and took out a soft zippered leather case from inside a small suitcase. He laid the leather case on the floor of the boot and opened it. A six-inch barrel nickel-plated .357 Colt Python was nestled inside. He looked at both of us. 'When we get there, I'm going in with you two. If we find Cox, I want to be in the house. Last time he had a gun to my head, but this time I'm going to blow off his fucking head with this.' Steve and I shared a look.

Thirty-six hours before

We were on the range at the Greenbank Army site undertaking our monthly weapons training. After lunch Don, the squad's senior sergeant, stopped the training to give us a Warning Order (the initial briefing for an upcoming operation). We would be raiding a farmhouse outside the western Queensland town of Boulia, some 1700 kilometres from Brisbane. 'Information has been received that Russell Cox is staying there with his girlfriend Helen Deane,' he announced.

Here we go, I thought, *Cox again*. Don was preparing an operation order for the job and we needed to be ready to go the next morning, but just as quickly we were stood down. This is how it often went with operations: one minute you'd be told to get kitted up for a job and the next you'd be told to stand down without reason or feedback. We were used to it.

Later that night Don contacted us once more. The job was on again and we were to be ready to be picked up at 5.00. We would be driving in convoy directly from Brisbane to a staging area near Windorah. From there we would regroup, go through the plan and launch an armed assault on the farmhouse.

By early 1986, Kathleen and I were living together. I'd turned down an invitation from a few of the boys to have post-training drinks, choosing instead to go home. Steve, on the other hand, led the charge to the pub. The next morning the police car we were to travel in picked me up and collected Steve along the way. It was 5.10 am, and he gingerly walked to the car, put his equipment bag in the boot, got inside and curled up in the corner to sleep most of the day.

It had now been almost nine years since Cox had escaped from Katingal and begun his spree of armed robberies. If he was living in this farmhouse he would undoubtedly be heavily armed, and the chances were high that he would actively resist arrest. I remembered the Hecker and Koch assault rifle he'd left behind when he narrowly eluded us after the Mayne Railway payroll operation.

These days, special weapons and tactical team operators would shudder at the plan we had been presented with. It was scant on detail. We were going to drive up a single driveway and launch an assault on the house, smashing our way straight through the front door while another assault team entered the house from the rear door and two other teams secured the perimeter. There was no isolate, contain and negotiate as you would today. This was also a time before distraction grenades (stun grenades) were used. We had no information about the layout of the target house so the only thing we could do was to figure it out on the spot as best we could. And while we generally had much better information regarding the floor plans and entry points than in this case, it was just the way it was.

We drove into Longreach at around 7.00 pm. The local police were expecting us but had not been told why. We received a full briefing from George Sharry, bought some food from a local road-house and grabbed a few hours' sleep while we could, leaving Longreach before midnight. The road changed from bitumen to unsealed roads with corrugations filled with the fine powdery bulldust familiar to any outback Queenslander. The dust stirred up by the vehicles hung in the dry air in clouds, forcing the cars to slow down to ensure the drivers could see far enough ahead. The police dogs weren't coping either and started to choke on the dust. We decided to stop for half an hour. The taste of bulldust in your mouth can only be tolerated for so long.

3.00 am, Friday 8 April 1986
After George had shown us his Colt Python revolver and announced his intention to blow off Cox's head, I looked at Steve. 'Mate,' I said quietly, 'we can't have him with us. Good bloke but he's not trained, and he could do something stupid, so that's not going to happen.'

Steve nodded slowly. 'I agree. He's a good bloke but he's not in the right head space to hit the house. That would be dangerous on a few fronts. How about we keep this to ourselves but make sure he's in one of the perimeter teams?'

'Good call,' I replied. 'Let me talk to the sniper team.' The snipers were to provide immediate perimeter security to the assault teams.

I organised for George to be positioned in the snipers' car and kept out of the way there. We'd deal with any blowback from him later but that would be better than having an untrained and angry man inside the house when we confronted Cox. While he out-ranked both Steve and me, I was an Emergency Squad assault team leader and my responsibility was to the safety of my team and, by extension, the occupants of the house including Cox.

We changed from our casual clothes into our black overalls and gathered our equipment. We were still a few hours away from the target, but it was time to start switching on. The convoy headed off again, carefully threading its way along the dirt road.

We reached the planned holding area a couple of hours later at the rising of the false dawn. This was the last stop, about ten kilo-metres from Cox's stronghold. All weapons were double checked and we went over the plan one last time. Unlike most of our plans, this one was scant on detail. We would drive at speed up the dirt road leading to the house and my team would be straight out of the car to force open the front door. The second assault team would go to the rear and force entry via the back door. It was impossible to nominate secondary points of entry without seeing the house. The sniper teams would follow and provide perimeter security in the event Cox or others started engaging us with gunfire as we approached.

Knowing George was safely tucked away with the perimeter team, I put him out of my mind as we drove closer. Steve and I were in the back seat of our car with two other assaulters in the front. The false dawn had gone, and the sun was starting to appear over the horizon as we opened the cattle gate about a kilometre from the house. Our driver floored it and we drove at high speed towards the target. The sound of our cars would have carried to the house well before we came into view, so there was no tactical advantage in travelling slowly.

Sheds were dotted around the traditional farmhouse, a couple of cars were parked in the yard and a small fence separated the yard from the rest of the property. We smashed through the small wooden fence and slid to a halt around three metres from the door. The familiar adrenaline surge coursed through me as we moved quickly to the front door, weapons up. Steve was first and he tried the handle. As we'd hoped it was unlocked, and he pushed it wide open as he brought his submachine gun to the aim position. I was right behind him. We moved inside, clearing each room as we made our way forward. The temptation in these jobs was to move with speed but it was vital that each area was checked to make sure no one was hiding to shoot you in the back as you passed. This had been drilled into us by the SAS at Battle Wing training each year.

I could hear the second assault team moving in from the rear of the house, clearing as they went. Within seconds, a man emerged from one of the rooms. He was wearing short pyjama bottoms and had an understandable look of alarm. 'What the fuck?' was as far as he got before Steve moved on him and grabbed him by the back of the neck, forcing him face down onto the floor. Steve planted his boot on the man's upper back to keep him in place as the other two of our assault team moved to secure him.

I kept covering the hallway when his wife emerged from the bedroom. She was angry and, somewhat disturbingly, naked. She was screaming at us like a banshee, using words that would make a sailor blush. We both moved past her to clear the bedroom as other team members secured her. Within a minute both teams had completely cleared the house.

The man and his woman were the only occupants of the house, although there were clear signs someone else had been living in a second bedroom. We waited for the detectives, led by George, to enter the house and take the two into custody.

As was required after each operation, we lined up and faced away from everyone else to unload, keeping our weapons pointed in a safe direction, in this case to the ground. We had been issued with Czech CZ 9 mm semi-automatic pistols as our secondary weapons. (Glocks would come later.) These CZs had an external hammer that was cocked back into single action when a bullet was chambered. This meant a very slight trigger pressure would fire the weapon. The only way to lower the hammer under control was by keeping hold of it with your left thumb and forefinger while squeezing the trigger. Unfortunately, this practice had resulted in a few unauthorised discharges (informally known as 'Fuck, what was that?') due to the hammer slipping out of one's grip. This was the main reason why Peter Kidd and I had driven the push for Glock pistols, which had no external hammer and were much safer to carry.

While unloading his pistol, Bob, who was the other assault team leader, lost control of the hammer and accidentally fired a shot. The round went harmlessly into the dirt. However, the real problem soon emerged from the house. The woman had broken free from the detective, who had draped a blanket over her. She burst through the front door and ran towards us screaming that we had murdered her husband. This of course was an understandable reaction, but as she was a rather large woman I just wish she'd kept the blanket on.

After the woman had been restrained and reunited with her very much alive and unharmed husband, Steve wryly announced to the team: 'Bob will do anything to get the attention of women. It'd be good if he was a bit choosier.'

We later learned that Cox the fox had done it again. Someone from headquarters had authorised police in a light plane to fly over the property a few days before our raid to look at the house. That was enough for Cox to pack up and leave. He didn't take any chances. I could understand that.

It was a long drive back to Brisbane, so we stopped at Charleville. Even though we were all dog tired, we booked into the local pub, cleaned up and went downstairs to spend a night drinking beer with the locals. George Sharry had forgiven us; I think he knew the decision to keep him out of the house was the right thing to do.

Cox stayed on the run until 1988, when he was captured at Melbourne's Doncaster Shoppingtown by the Victoria Police Armed Robbery Squad. His days of freedom were over. Like many veteran cops, I still have respect for him. He was a professional, you have to admire that. So were we, but the difference was that he got his rush from robbing banks, we got our rush by chasing men like him.

ROCKY

There are some people along the journey who touch your life in ways you never expect and never forget. Rocky was one of those.

Being a cop requires you to have some emotional detachment, otherwise you'd quickly collapse under the weight of what you see and experience. It's a fine line because you don't want to lose your humanity along the way. I'd been given excellent advice by an older detective when I was a junior cop: 'You can start off being a nice guy and turn into a bastard if you have to, but you can't go the other way, it doesn't work.' I took his advice and tried to treat people (civilians, police and crooks) as I found them. I'd start off being a nice guy . . . unless, of course, they were bastards of the highest order, then it was quite acceptable to be the bad guy.

It was late July in 1986, a couple of weeks after our annual Canungra course, and I was sitting in Harry Edwards' office with Dennis. As well as being a part-time Emergency Squad member, Dennis was also an experienced covert operator with the secretive Bureau of Criminal Intelligence. This closed-door briefing was on a strictly need-to-know basis.

A witness, Rocky, had been relocated to Brisbane from Sydney for protection from a probable mafia-backed hit. The witness and several other men had been hired by mafia figures as crop sitters to supervise the cultivation of a large marijuana crop in northern Queensland. They had spent six months living rough in the bush.

When the crop was harvested one of the other crop sitters had ripped a few pounds off the top, and when this theft was discovered the man had been murdered in Sydney on the orders of the same mafia figures who had hired them.

Our witness had a crisis of conscience and provided a state-ment to the New South Wales Homicide Squad. As a result, he'd had a serious and credible threat made against his life. Our job was to keep him safe until he attended the committal hearing in Townsville and gave evidence regarding the principals behind the cultivation of the crop. After that he would probably need protec-tion in the lead up to the murder trial in Sydney, but that wouldn't be our problem.

The briefing was simple: we were to select a team from the Emergency Squad and put in place twenty-four-hour protection for the witness. Dennis had been given the responsibility of running this job and he had selected me as his number two.

'Be careful with this,' Harry said to both of us. 'Make sure you get the right crew and keep your eyes open.' I wasn't fazed by the job, I had that familiar excitement of being part of a risky oper-ation, of doing something away from the normal day to day.

We went into the armoury and drew two Heckler and Koch MP5 submachine guns and two short-barrelled folding stock shotguns as well as enough ammunition to take over a small country. We had already been issued with 9mm semi-automatic pistols as part of our regular Emergency Squad roles, but we wanted to supplement those pistols with better weapons. Just in case.

We loaded everything into a white transit van with heavily tinted windows and drove to a side street near the drab, four-storey

CIB headquarters in Makerston Street. Dennis had specifically asked for me because he knew he could trust me. We'd both been undercover agents and knew the importance of being able to trust your partners.

We met Rocky in a secure office in the Drug Squad. He was sitting at a scarred wooden table, chain-smoking. He had a strong handshake but avoided eye contact, like a cattle dog that had been kicked too much and expected it to happen again at any time. Rocky was a second-generation Italian–Australian and had grown up in Mt Druitt, one of the roughest areas in Sydney. He was 172 centimetres, strongly built with a barrel chest and broad shoulders and had short black receding hair, sideburns and a soul patch under his bottom lip. He looked to be in his mid-twenties.

We introduced ourselves and told him we'd be looking after him from now on. Dennis sat down opposite. 'The main thing is you do exactly what we tell you, no arguments. We'll do our best to make it as comfortable as we can.'

Rocky looked up and for the first time I saw the uncertainty in his eyes. He nodded slowly, as if accepting his fate. I could see he needed to hear he was safe, because he had probably had very little to do with police in a positive way. 'No one will get to you, Rocky. We're here to make sure of it. This is what we're good at.'

Rocky looked back at me and didn't reply. He just picked up his duffel bag, which stored the only belongings he had, and stood waiting to be told what to do.

It was a highly secretive operation for good reason. As I'd found out with 'Joe from Griffith' and other undercover jobs, not everyone could be trusted and the rule of need to know was the best and safest approach. Nobody else outside a tight circle knew any details about Rocky, and the extent of our briefing was limited to keeping him safe before his attendance in the Townsville court. The committal hearing date hadn't been set, so that meant keeping him under armed guard every hour of the day for as long as it took.

Nothing had been arranged, it was up to us to do what needed to be done. We stayed in a Brisbane motel for a few days while trying to find a suitable place to rent, taking turns watching Rocky. Eventually we found an isolated house in Mt Nebo, in the Brisbane hinterland. The plan was to get Rocky settled in an area where the comings and goings of a twenty-four-hour protection team wouldn't draw attention. Tactically we also needed somewhere that would allow us to see anyone approaching, either in a vehicle or on foot. This place was perfect.

To get to the house we had to travel along the winding Mt Nebo Road lined with rainforest and find the almost hidden driveway entrance nestled among the gum trees. The unsealed driveway led past another house, then down along a dirt road for a hundred metres or so. Bushland surrounded the property, so the only way in by vehicle was down that single track. Isolation and limited access points were the most important aspects we needed, and the site we'd chosen had both. Standing behind the house, you couldn't hear anything except the birds, and you couldn't see anything other than scrub and open sky. It was going to be a culture shock for a boy from Sydney's busy and crowded Mt Druitt.

There was no real estate agent involved; Dennis had dealt directly with the owner of the house. Harry Edwards was the only other person to know the address and we trusted him completely. Today, this would be a tightly controlled and well-resourced operation, but back then there was no defined witness protection program. We were the first members of the Queensland Police to undertake a job like this, and probably among the first in Australia.

Witness protection would evolve very quickly in the following few years as witnesses called before the Fitzgerald Inquiry rolled over on each other like beach balls in the wind.

———

As we drove up Mt Nebo Road to the house that would become very familiar over the next months, Rocky started to relax a little with us. 'This is a lot like the area around Gumlu where the crop was,' he said, looking out the window. 'Really pretty. I like the rainforest. Different from where I grew up.'

'Me too,' I replied. 'I grew up in the bush with red dust everywhere.'

'Yeah? I thought you grew up in the city, the way you talk.'

I smiled. This wasn't the first time I'd heard that. If only people knew what my childhood had been, they'd be more than a little surprised.

Dennis stopped the van beside the house. It wasn't huge, but it didn't need to be. There were two bedrooms upstairs, one for Rocky and a spare, and a living area downstairs. Dennis and I let Rocky get used to his new home while we took stock of the area. We checked the access points, and the state of the doors and windows. Then we sat down and mapped out an emergency evacuation plan, as well as an action plan in case anyone from Rocky's former life tracked him down.

There were no procedures to follow. We just figured it out as we went along. The rule we lived by was '*Hope for the best and plan for the worst.*' We couldn't be certain that Rocky's location would be kept secret forever and we had to look at all scenarios. We established where we'd take cover, where we'd shoot from, under what circumstances we would fire and how we'd get Rocky out. We plotted an escape route through the bush to the main road, and checked all our equipment, firearms, radios and vehicle. Mobile phones wouldn't become available in Australia for another year, so we were totally reliant on fixed-line phones and radios.

Necessity is the mother of invention. Without electronic alarms and sensors, night-vision technology and security cameras, we used an old army trick and strung up empty beer cans on fishing wire between saplings on likely approaches to camp to provide some sort of alarm.

Dennis and I stayed with Rocky day and night for the next two weeks. If we needed supplies, one of us would go out while the other stayed at the house. Rocky was polite enough and after the first few days he started to relax more. I saw the first signs of his sense of humour emerging and I found myself starting to like him.

Over that fortnight, we personally selected a team from the Emergency Squad to support us. We needed reliable operators who could keep their cool if shots were fired. The squad wasn't yet full time, so we had to wait for the men to be released from their stations and we didn't always get our first choices. The committal hearing in Townsville was a few months away and no one wanted to lose officers from their stations for that long. When the team was finally ready, Dennis left me with Rocky for the day while he drove down to Petrie Terrace to brief the team.

When I look back now, that was the day Rocky and I really started to get to know each other. I had been warned about empathising with targets before, but I'd been an undercover cop and was more comfortable than most in that world. Besides, I'd met drug dealers who had a better sense of morality than some of the cops I knew, so those warnings meant little to me. I made some tea and we sat at the old kitchen table surrounded by bushland and silence. I asked him how he was doing. He looked across the brim of his cup and chuckled. 'Not the best I've been, mate. Never thought I'd be spending all my time with cops. No offence.' I smiled back. 'None taken. I don't like all cops either, believe me. But the ones coming today are good blokes. Just be yourself.'

Rocky visibly brightened as he talked about his parents and the rest of his family. Mt Druitt was one of the toughest suburbs in Sydney and he'd learned street smarts from an early age. Like a lot of others, his journey to offending had started with stealing from the corner shop, taking cars for joyrides and breaking into the occasional factory. He'd had normal jobs from time to time but had fallen in with a bunch of minor crooks and progressed to doing some enforcement for some organised crooks. 'I'm a boxer, mate. You don't have to hit anybody if you've got the right look and attitude. Just blokes who owed money, you just turn up and tell 'em to pay up.'

His father worked at the markets and his mother was a cleaner. He'd been raised as a Catholic and I could see he still had the guilt of most of the Catholics I'd met, even those who'd lapsed.

I told him about my unhappy and violent childhood, about growing up in caravan parks, moving from town to town to go where the work was, and how it always seemed like I was getting belted at each new school and then beaten at home. It just seemed normal to me. I remember Rocky shaking his head in disbelief and sadness.

I was no longer the armed cop. We were two young men getting to know each other.

We talked about music, and women, and sport and life generally. We were both fans of Cold Chisel and were convinced that 'Khe Sanh' should be the national anthem. As we talked I reflected on how differently my life could have turned out. I saw in Rocky what could have become of me.

Towards dusk we heard the van turn off the road and make its way down the dirt track towards us. Rocky extended his hand. 'I enjoyed today, mate,' I said.

'So did I, Keithy.' I was now Keithy. I liked it.

Four new team members walked in through the back of the house. Dennis introduced them all to Rocky. I could see immediately that not all of them would share my understanding of Rocky. Rob and Russ were from the school of black-and-white policing: Rocky was a bad guy, and they were cops. I had no doubt that they would protect him to the best of their ability, but they weren't about to get to know him as a person. No judgement from me, everyone is different, but it was going to make Rocky's life challenging.

There were now six of us working on Operation Rocky, two per twelve-hour shift. Over the following weeks Rocky did his best to be engaging and friendly. He was funny and good company. But you can only stay put in a house and watch television for so long. Rocky was losing his fitness and developing a bad case of cabin fever. We had an unmarked car as well as the van, so when we could Dennis and I would take Rocky for a drive into the township of Mt Nebo for a cup of coffee. Sometimes we'd travel down the winding road to Brisbane and show him the sights, as best we could. Occasionally we'd go to CIB headquarters, where Drug Squad detective Bruce Horton would talk to Rocky about the brief of evidence. I liked Bruce very much; he wasn't like most detectives I knew. For a start, he didn't dress like his grandfather and he had a genuine concern for Rocky.

I still had no idea about the details that had led Rocky into witness protection apart from the fact that one of his associates had been murdered and he might be next. I didn't want to ask directly and knew he'd tell me when he was ready.

———

A couple of months into the job, Dennis was rotated back to the Bureau of Criminal Intelligence (BCI). They couldn't spare him any longer. I was still second in charge.

The management of the operation was handed to a detective sergeant from the secretive Special Branch. No one outside the Special Branch really knew what they did apart from keeping tabs on political activists. That was typical of the Bjelke-Petersen regime in 1980s Queensland, having police monitor and disrupt anti-government agitators. Armed with cameras and clipboards, Special Branch officers had been present at every street march and demonstration that had taken place since my swearing in as a junior cop in 1977. The more public part of their job was to provide close protection for the premier and selected VIPs, and that was why this detective sergeant had been given the job of managing protection for Rocky. In reality, all he did was sign overtime forms and speak to me about once a month. The day-to-day operation was under my control.

Before Dennis went back to the BCI, we had agreed to take Rocky out from time to time to have a beer in a quiet pub in Enoggera, a working-class suburb not far from the city centre. Rocky had been like a little kid on an outing. He'd been locked up with us for weeks and it was probably the best thing we could have done for his mental health.

When we saw how much this had boosted Rocky's spirits, Dennis and I decided this should be a frequent occurrence. Most of the team were happy to kick in for Rocky's food and beers given we were making a lot of overtime, but Rob didn't approve. I didn't care. In my view, taking Rocky out of the house helped keep him happy and almost guaranteed he wouldn't just pack up and leave. After all, he wasn't under arrest; he was in the safe house voluntarily as a witness.

Life went on with one day blending into the next until one afternoon when Rocky decided to tell me his story.

'Anyone told you about what happened to me, Keithy?' he asked apropos of nothing as we went for a walk to get some fresh air.

I looked at him and shook my head. 'No, mate.' I knew to keep quiet. I'd used that approach often enough in formal police interviews; it was a human trait to fill the silence.

He took a deep breath. 'Going to the cops was fucking hard, mate. It was against everything I'd ever known. You don't talk to the cops where I come from.'

He'd been offered a job by someone he knew to sit on a marijuana crop in north Queensland. Rocky had never been outside Sydney and the job would net him ten thousand dollars, a fortune in those days. He and five others would have to stay there for four months or so to take care of the plants and maintain the crop.

'It sounded so good I said yes straight away.' Rocky looked at the rainforest and gums that stretched around us in all directions. The only sound was the birdsong. 'It was a lot like this, but hotter.'

They lived in a bush camp for the duration with occasional trips into Gumlu for supplies. When the crop was harvested the plants were dried for transport. It was over the couple of weeks while the plants were drying that one of the men had taken some of the harvest and hidden it.

'I told him not to do it, but he didn't think anyone would find out. Stupid bastard.' Rocky didn't want any part of it; it was the wrong thing to do. 'They paid us to do a job and it wasn't right to rip off anything.'

The dried plants were collected in trucks and Rocky and the others were flown back to Sydney to go their separate ways. A couple of weeks later Rocky was told to go to a house in Rooty Hill and to hire a car on his way there. 'I thought they had another job for me, so I did what I was told. You don't fuck around with these blokes. You know who they were, right?'

'No, mate, I don't,' I lied.

He almost whispered the words, as if the trees around us were full of eavesdroppers. 'The mafia, Keithy. The mafia.'

When Rocky knocked on the door, he was taken to the kitchen table. Three men he hadn't yet met were sitting there. They were friendly enough at first, but then they asked him where the missing dope had gone and warned him that he would only have one chance to tell the truth.

'I was shitting myself,' Rocky said. 'I knew they were fucking serious. I told them what had happened. Everything. I've never been so scared. When I finished talking, the boss just nodded at me and said they already knew everything, they just wanted to see if I'd bullshit them. One of them gave me a beer and told me to leave the car there. He said I'd need to pick it up the next afternoon. I drank my beer and left. I didn't want to ask any questions, I just wanted to get out.'

When Rocky returned to the house at Rooty Hill the next day, the sides of the car were covered in mud and the windows were spattered with grime. He was told to clean the car and take it back to the hire company. He did what he was told.

'Cleaning the outside was okay,' Rocky said. 'But then I opened up the boot to vacuum it out. There was blood in the boot, mate,' he said after a long pause. 'They killed my mate and used the car to take him somewhere and bury him. Some of the blood must have leaked out when they wrapped him up.'

Rocky finished cleaning the car and drove it back to the rental company. Helping to cover up for a murder was the heaviest thing he'd ever done. He worried whether this was another test or whether the mafia was using him to cover its tracks. After all, the car was in his name. Was he being punished because he hadn't stopped the rip off? He couldn't come to terms with the fact that his mate had been murdered for something like this.

Rocky and I walked back inside the house. I broke my own rule about not drinking on duty and grabbed a couple of beers from the fridge. I handed one to Rocky as we sat at the kitchen table.

'I couldn't sleep, I couldn't eat. All I kept thinking about is that they killed my mate and buried him somewhere in the bush. In the end I went to a priest at my local church. I made confession, I had to.'

The priest advised Rocky to tell the police. He wrestled with the idea for a couple of days, but in the end he made a trip into the city, well away from Mt Druitt, and walked into a police station. Within minutes the Homicide Squad was alerted, and Rocky was taken into protective custody. He'd been allowed to see his parents and they had both cried.

'My dad told me he was proud of me and I was doing the right thing,' Rocky said, his eyes filling with tears. Then he grinned. 'So that's how I got here hanging around with cops.'

'Could be worse, mate,' I shrugged. 'You could be hanging around with lawyers.'

What he had done took balls of steel. This kind of courage is highly respected by cops. But his reward was to spend his days with armed men he barely knew. I felt that the least we could do was try to make him feel comfortable.

I'd been able to persuade the Task Force senior sergeant to let Ando and Giblet do some shifts with us. He wouldn't let them join the witness protection team permanently as he still needed them for Task Force work. Because they had both been undercover like me, they were very comfortable with Rocky and saw the man, not the history.

Rocky bonded with them quickly. It didn't hurt that Ando knew a lot of pretty women and he insisted on taking Rocky to meet them. Nothing sexual happened but I know Rocky was happier being with them than he was with us. The problem was we couldn't tell anyone who Rocky really was. Ando and I decided the best story was that Rocky was a New South Wales detective on a secret operation with us. The girls loved it and he loved playing the game.

———

In the old days, a police badge was a key to the city. It made sense to keep the cops onside, so they were welcomed to every nightclub in town. Give them free entry and they'd drink twice as much as anyone else, so the loss on the cover charge was immaterial. The Underground nightclub was located across the road from what is now Suncorp Stadium and was the place to be in Brisbane's nightlife scene. It was where the beautiful people (and there were quite a few) tended to congregate. Ando and I had spent a lot of time there in the past and one of the bouncers was a student in the taekwondo class Ando taught. Rocky loved the whole deal. No lining up; we'd just walk to the front of the line and be ushered inside. It was a world he'd never experienced and was light years away from the pubs in Mt Druitt.

Two of us were always on duty. I was firm with my instructions to the team that there was no drinking while we were rostered on. The threat to his life was credible and we needed to keep focused. (Once the rostered shift was over and the new team took over, however, it was a different matter.) Rocky didn't go to the bar alone, didn't take a piss alone. We knew he wouldn't try to slip away, but it was a high-risk situation so we were always armed. We'd wear jeans, a T-shirt and a leather jacket, and carry a 9 mm semi-automatic pistol in a shoulder holster with spare magazines on the other side. We grew our hair and only shaved every couple of days. With his neat soul patch and short hair, Rocky was the most presentable of us all.

It's easy to spot a bunch of cops out for the night once you know what to look for. They're the ones in a tight circle not talking to anyone else. They'll be drinking as much as anyone and they'll laugh more, but nobody will break into the unit unless they want them there. Police see and do things that most people can never imagine, and the camaraderie created by those experiences closes others out. With Rocky as part of the group it was even more important that no one else joined us.

One night Rocky and I were at the Underground and wanted to hear 'Khe Sanh'. It was 1.30 in the morning and the place was packed. I made my way upstairs through the dance floor to the DJ booth. I knew Kelvin quite well and he was happy to see me.

'Hey, how you going, mate? Come in, what can I do for you?' he asked.

'Great, Kelvin,' I said. 'Quick request, mate. Can you play 'Khe Sanh'?'

He held up a piece of paper with a long list of scrawled song titles. 'Sorry, Keith, I've got about twenty bloody requests lined up. I can do it, but it'll have to wait.'

I didn't respond. I just held eye contact with him, slowly reached under my jacket and pulled out my pistol. I placed it on the bench beside the turntables. Kelvin looked at the pistol and back to me, wide-eyed.

'I don't think you quite understood me,' I said. Then I grinned.

Kelvin burst into laughter. He'd always been pretty laid back. 'You're right, what was I thinking, you mad bastard?' He dug through his records. A moment later the opening riff of the 'real' national anthem filled the room.

I put my pistol back in its holster and patted Kelvin on the arm. 'Thanks very much, mate. Cheers, have a good night.' He nodded a few times, chuckled to himself and sorted through the collection of records.

From then on, whenever I went to the Underground and Kelvin was the DJ he played 'Khe Sanh'. I'd look up and he'd give me a thumbs up.

———

We'd taken a risk by showing Rocky Brisbane's nightlife (and broken rules, not for the first time), but the improvement in his mood was well worth it. He was brighter and happier. Although it wasn't our job to keep him happy, it was the right thing to do for him as a person and to ensure he would be around to give evidence.

I started to look forward to my twelve-hour shifts. Apart from having to be constantly vigilant to the threat environment, it was like spending the day with your mate. And because it was convenient, I often arranged to do a late shift followed by an early morning shift, which meant sleeping at the safe house. I was almost spending more time with Rocky than I was with Kathleen.

She wasn't impressed, but that was the life of being a cop's partner.

I'd come to know people on the other side of the law when I was an undercover operative but had never revealed my real self to any of them. I'd even liked some of them but with Rocky it was different. And although we were from different worlds, neither of us hid anything about ourselves from the other. We were around the same age and I often wondered if I'd have followed a similar path to his had the lottery of life not given me an ability to succeed academically, opening doors that were closed to him.

Rocky had started boxing as a kid, initially to learn how to defend himself on the street. Then he competed in amateur fights, ending up with a couple of amateur titles. The problem was that boxing also attracted the criminal element. That was how he'd become tied up with the mafia associates. Along the way, he'd made some easy money with debt collection. Showing me his debt collector scowl, he explained: 'It's like boxing, Keithy, you don't have to hate the other bloke, but you have to look like you do. That's part of the science. The other part is how to use the ring and throw combos.' He was on his feet, floating around the room throwing jab, and cross, hook and uppercut combinations. I saw how it made his eyes brighter and brought a smile to his face.

'I really miss training, mate. I really do. I've gotta get off the smokes and do something. I'm going to shit'. He was right. He'd put on weight and was drinking and smoking a lot more than when I first met him. This gave me an idea.

The following day I made a call and told Rocky to grab his training gear. I was rostered with John, one of the original team. We drove from the house directly to the Fortitude Valley Police Boys' Club. A mate of ours was in charge and he was happy for Rocky to train there however he wanted. He spent the first visit skipping and hitting the heavy bag for an hour. He was exhausted but couldn't stop smiling. Whenever I was rostered, we would make a visit to the club a regular part of our day. That's what mates do.

When Rob was on a shift Rocky's movements were restricted, and he was confined to the house. Rob still thought we were too friendly with Rocky. He saw the world as black and white, very much like I had when I first left the academy, before undercover had changed my world. Rob couldn't get past Rocky's background and couldn't see how cooperating with the police showed Rocky's character much more than his history of petty crime. I don't doubt that Rob would have protected Rocky if things had turned to shit, and in that way he would have performed the job perfectly. But in my view the job was much more than that, and I believed Rocky deserved to be treated as a person, not a captive.

One day, by the good graces of a certain member of the team who may or may not have been a former undercover, Rocky came into possession of a small amount of pot. The consensus with most of the guys was that if it chilled him out, or just put him in a good frame of mind, then we didn't have a problem. Rob wasn't happy about it, so I told Rocky not to smoke when he was rostered on.

Eventually Rocky asked if he could grow his own plants. He said, 'If I grow my own, I won't have to wait for anyone to find some for me.'

'Well, let's face it, you've got the experience,' I said. We both laughed at that.

My undercover background had markedly changed my view of the rights and wrongs of cannabis use. Cultivating cannabis was against the law in Queensland, but I knew plenty of people, including one or two cops, who grew a small plant in their backyard without hurting anyone. They were hardly Mexican drug cartels. I also figured that Rocky and therefore the whole operation would be better off if we made a few small concessions, even if they weren't completely according to Hoyle.

I told him to go ahead if he had a few seeds, just not to be obvious.

A few weeks later I arrived at the house to find Rob and John watching television downstairs. John looked over as I walked inside and he greeted me with a roll of his eyes. 'G'day, Keith. Rocky's upstairs. You might want to go and have a chat.'

Rocky's door was closed. I knocked and went in. He was lying on the bed staring at the ceiling.

'How's it going, mate?'

'That cunt downstairs,' he said, his voice emotionless, 'broke all my plants.'

I knew exactly who he was talking about. Those plants meant a lot to Rocky and, even though it was unlikely they'd ever yield any results, he enjoyed tending to them.

'You know the rest of us don't mind what you do,' I said. 'But there's nothing we can do about him. He doesn't see things like we do.'

'I know, Keithy. I don't have a problem with you guys.'

I went back downstairs and smoothed things over with Rob. I was pissed off about it, but the law was on his side. It was a case of two conflicting ideologies. I told Rob I'd take the morning shift, so he didn't need to come back for a couple of days.

He was happy to leave early, and the tension dissipated the second the door closed behind him. John would stay until Ando arrived for our shift.

I went outside to check the surroundings and to think about what had happened. Rocky would get over it. What choice did he have? He was living in the bush with men he'd never met before and would never have imagined being friendly with. On one level Rob's actions had probably reinforced Rocky's view of police, although I knew he wouldn't judge Ando and me as a result. This was part of the ambiguity between the law and how we operated in and around it. I was happy to bend rules; sometimes the best outcomes weren't strictly in adherence with the letter of the law. In the world of undercover following the rules could get you badly hurt. Letting Rocky have a joint or grow a couple of plants was against the law, but in my view it was harmless. It was a fine line to walk, and I knew full well that if the bosses knew they'd hang me out to dry. Rocky was a witness to a cold blooded and ruthless murder. I was happy to take the chance.

Like me, Ando genuinely liked Rocky and would hang out with the on-duty team on his nights off. Rocky's curiosity about being a cop was insatiable. He always wanted to hear about the car chases and the brawls, but more than anything he loved hearing about the moronic senior cops who didn't know how to manage people. When I told him about the time our disciplinarian inspector George Small was booked on the air and was greeted by an anonymous voice saying 'George Small is a cunt', he was in tears of laughter.

———

The date for the committal hearing in the Townsville Magistrates Court had finally come. The prosecution would be providing evidence, including witness testimony, before the magistrate decided if the evidence was sufficient to warrant a trial in a higher court in front of a judge and jury.

Rocky had been with us for almost four months by then. We all flew to Townsville in the police plane and spent a week at a hotel where we had arranged to rent the entire floor for better security. The New South Wales Homicide Squad detectives had also flown up to support Rocky. They were as genuinely happy to see him as he was to see them. I wondered whether it was because he'd become used to cops by now, or whether they were a familiar connection to his hometown. Either way, it was good to see him laugh.

Each night we were in Townsville we had dinner with the New South Wales blokes and maybe a beer, depending on our rostered shift status. One night when I was at the bar and Rocky was just being himself, one of the New South Wales detectives turned to me and said, 'See that little bloke, Banksy?'

'You mean Rocky?' I replied.

'Yes mate, Rocky. He's got more balls than most coppers I know. That's why we like him. Just make sure you look after him, he deserves it.' I understood exactly what he meant.

Rocky gave his evidence like a pro. The magistrate committed the defendants to stand trial in the Supreme Court on charges of large-scale cannabis cultivation.

———

As happens with a lot of witnesses after they give evidence, Rocky started to doubt his decision to testify. He'd lost sight of the reasons he'd gone into protection in the first place. He missed the life he once had and felt guilty about giving evidence. It was hard to remove the ingrained attitude he'd been taught all his life of not cooperating with the cops.

Rocky and I talked about it a lot in those last days after we'd returned to the safe house, sitting on the lounge or on the back porch when it was hot. The psychological pressure to change his situation was mounting, stemming from the circumstances he was living in and from those he'd left behind in Sydney. I thought it was inevitable that he'd want to go back, but what provoked his decision was an instruction from the assistant commissioner to downgrade his protection status.

It was a budget issue. Renting the house at Mt Nebo and utilising Emergency Squad members on overtime rates was now seen to be too great an expense to pay. In the end a decision was made to move him into a cheaper weatherboard house in an inner suburb of Brisbane.

It was also decided that his protection detail would include some non-tactical personnel—in other words, general police. That eliminated the overtime cost, but it meant there were men on the team who had probably only fired their service revolvers a couple of times before, if at all. I fought the decision. There were too many access points to the new house, it was too central, it was easy to breach, anti-surveillance was difficult and the team wasn't trained. I was told to stop complaining or I'd be removed from the protection detail.

The move increased the risk and Rocky knew it. He could tell the police command didn't want to spend money on him and that made him feel worthless. About six weeks after we moved to the new house, he phoned his mother from a nearby phone box. As soon as I walked into the house the following day, he said he had something to tell me.

'Keithy, I've got to go back,' he said. 'My mother says they've been in touch and given her and my dad their word.' I took a breath.

'She said they've forgiven me as long as I don't give evidence at the trial.'

I explained how unrealistic the proposition was. I told him I was worried about him and that I thought it was a set up. We talked about what happened to his mate, the whole reason he was in witness protection in the first place. But he desperately wanted to believe they were telling the truth. He wanted to hear that all was forgiven and that he could go home.

The last time I saw Rocky was at the bus terminal in Roma Street opposite police headquarters. I wanted to be the one to take him there, to try to talk him out of it one more time. We shook hands and said our goodbyes. We had no power to hold him and he'd made up his mind to go home. Six months earlier, we'd met as a cop and a witness. In that time he'd become more than a job, he was a good mate. I was going to miss him.

A few months later, the Drug Squad received information from the Sydney Homicide Squad that Rocky had been flown to Italy by the mafia family he'd returned to. Shortly after he arrived, his body had been found by Italian police with two gunshots to the back of the head. I wasn't surprised, but I was incredibly sad. In my heart I knew that it would end up like this. I often wonder what his last thoughts were. I only hope his end was quick.

We organised a private wake at the Paddington Hotel, just those of us who had looked after Rocky. Not everyone attended. Later that night, after the others had gone, Ando and I shared a quiet toast to him. This shouldn't have happened to a good bloke who trusted too easily. But I was coming to understand by then that there was no 'supposed to'. The universe is chaotic.

I don't know who made the decision to downgrade Rocky's protection status, and I don't know their reasoning. In more cynical moments I suspect that he'd used up his value to Queensland Police when he gave his evidence. But then, incompetence can look like callousness. In some ways Queensland Police was a ramshackle operation and those in charge may have simply miscalculated the risk.

Today I look back at that time and am struck by how big the divide was between the work of everyday police and the ingrained culture of the institution. Some of its attitudes hadn't changed since the 1950s; its lack of worldliness and accountability endangered us and the people under our protection. It was this that had pushed Rocky to return to Sydney.

I left the Paddington Hotel that night with the same respect I still hold for police on the front line, but my attitude towards the police department itself was changing. From working as 'meat on the hoof' (undercover), to the attempted bribes and lack of support and now this, the death of a brave man, it was hard to keep on seeing the Queensland Police as I had done when I joined. I had believed it was there to keep the people of Queensland safe, without fear or favour. I wasn't so sure anymore.

COURSES AND MORE

It had been a big year, 1986. I'd already trained as a bomb technician and been part of the first witness protection operation for
Queensland and now I was going to spend a couple of weeks in
Sydney with a few other squad operators undertaking a course
on aircraft assault. The New South Wales Special Weapons and
Operations Squad (SWOS) had invited Queensland to send a team
of tactical operators to learn the fine art of launching an assault on
a Boeing 747 in the event of a terrorist hijacking and I was one of
the lucky ones chosen.

In the 1970s and 1980s, terrorism had frequently involved
hijackings. Part of each state and territory's response to terrorist
acts was to contain the situation until the arrival of the SAS. In real
terms, however, it would take the Perth-based SAS hours to reach
the east coast and, if the shit hit the fan, we needed to be able to
launch an assault and save the hostages.

That's how we found ourselves at Sydney airport every day for
two weeks practising assaults on a Boeing 747 simulator hidden out
of sight in an aircraft hangar. The primary task of our training was
to save the lives of hostages. We were taught various ways of getting
inside an aircraft and to engage the terrorists, the gentle term for
shooting them dead if necessary. To err on the side of caution, and

just as I did with my bomb technician training, I am not going to write about our training in detail, even though it was a long time ago.

The course also gave us the chance to further strengthen the tactical network across borders. Queensland was a year or so behind New South Wales and Victoria in setting up a full-time tactical squad. Peter Kidd was still the only full-time member in Brisbane, but the plan remained to increase that number by mid-1987. Like us, most of the SWOS members were part time, but there was a core of ten or so operators who were permanent. I'd become good friends with two of them, John and Angus, who had attended the Canungra Battle Wing camp with us earlier that year. Our paths would continue to cross in the years to come.

I came back to the office in Brisbane in time to work in the Task Force over the Christmas and New Year period. This involved the usual round of festive activities such as punching on with and arresting pissed and violent groups of young men with whom we crossed paths.

One Friday night leading up to Christmas, Ando and I were with the Task Force crew in Surfers Paradise dealing with several men near Cavill Avenue. One of them took a dislike to me and decided the best way to deal with his feelings was to punch me in the face. I had been quite affronted by this behaviour and beat him to it. The problem was that my counter punch landed squarely on his mouth and one of his incisors penetrated my knuckle. He was placed in the back of a nearby police van and later charged at the Southport watchhouse. I thought no more of it until a few hours later when we were driving back to the Police Depot in Brisbane and my hand began throbbing with pain.

I took painkillers but by the morning my hand was badly swollen. Researchers assert the male brain doesn't mature until around the age of twenty-six. It was probably later than that for me because I didn't think about seeing a doctor and certainly didn't consider not going to work. That would have been too sensible. Kathleen bathed my hand and I lied and said it felt fine. We were working the Gold Coast again that night at a Midnight Oil concert and I wasn't going to miss that, infected hand or not.

That night Greeny, one of the Taskies, was grappling with a concert goer, losing his footing and being pushed through a barbed wire fence. I drove Greeny to the Southport Hospital and while I was there, I asked a nurse for some pain relief. She took one look at my hand and immediately hospitalised me for a severe infection. An orthopaedic surgeon was called and the next day I was in surgery. If I hadn't been admitted that night and undergone surgery, the surgeon later told me, I probably would have lost my little finger and perhaps half my hand.

The lesson I took from this was simple: don't punch anyone in the mouth, aim for the jaw. And, if you are in pain, it's probably a good idea to see a doctor.

———

The Emergency Squad was quickly evolving into almost a permanent role for me. We were being activated more and more to conduct high-risk raids. Over the first quarter of 1987, we performed scores of these types of jobs. We learned from our mistakes and continually improved. There was no rule book, and a lot of our tactics were learned through trial and error. Breaching strongholds wasn't just a matter of using a sledgehammer on a door, for example; there were various ways of getting inside. The key to everything was the element of surprise.

I took great satisfaction in being part of an assault team conducting house entries on armed robbers and being able to give violent criminals a taste of their own medicine. Imagine for a moment that you're an armed robber who gets a buzz from holding up a bank, terrorising bank staff and customers and racing off with bags of money. Then, one morning you're suddenly woken in your bed to find four men in balaclavas and black overalls pointing guns at your head. It was amazing how many of those 'tough guys' whimpered and cringed when they were at the wrong end of a shotgun. It was our way of getting revenge on behalf of all those frightened bank tellers who might never recover from the experience of being held up.

On one job we stormed a two-storey unit in the inner-city suburb of New Farm. (A place of massage parlours, illegal casinos, unlicensed liquor venues, street prostitutes and strip clubs, New Farm would feature prominently in the Fitzgerald Inquiry, which would bring down the state government and its police commissioner.) We were looking for a wanted armed robber. Simultaneously we smashed through the front door and a second-floor window to find one of the targets was happily brushing his teeth in front of the bathroom mirror. Within ten seconds he had been grabbed, passed down the staircase by two of the assault team operators, cable tied and pushed to the floor to sit with his back to the wall. It all happened so quickly that his toothbrush was still sticking out of his mouth.

In April of that year, Harry Edwards told me I'd been selected to attend the Police Counter Terrorist Instructors Course at the SAS barracks in Swanbourne, Western Australia. I'd be going over with Gordon, an Emergency Squad member from Townsville, and Bob, a sniper from the Brisbane squad. Peter Kidd had done the course the year before and he'd loved every minute of it. I knew then and there that I'd made the right choice in agreeing to join the Task Force. My dream had become a reality.

The Task Force was officially disbanded on 10 May 1987 and the full-time Tactical Response Group (TRG) was created in its place. We relocated from Petrie Terrace to the Police Depot at Alderley. Our offices were inside a large hangar that housed not only us, but other support services including the Dog Squad. We finally had our own place.

In June Gordon, Bob and I flew to Perth. We were met at the airport by members of the Perth TRG and taken to Campbell Barracks, located right on one of the most scenic beaches in Perth. I was greeted by the sight of Jim Venn from the Victorian SOG and John and Angus from New South Wales' SWOS. 'Banksy, get a haircut ya poof,' Venny boomed. My disdain for regulation haircuts was a constant source of amusement for him.

The camaraderie of tactical teams across the country is hard to describe. In that world there were no state or territory rivalries. We were all one team, and it was good to see mates again.

The next two weeks were intense and some of the best of my life. The snipers were issued with their rifles and went off each morning to their range. As assaulters, we were issued with our own Heckler and Koch submachine guns for the duration of the course. We'd also brought our personal handguns and equipment, but everything else we needed was supplied. We started each day with a long run along the beach followed by sessions with the SAS physical training wing.

The course objective was to qualify us as Police Assault Group counter-terrorist instructors under the National Anti-Terrorist Plan as it was then. As with the bomb course, funding was provided by the federal government and the instructors were experienced SAS operators, some of whom had trained with UK and USA Special Forces as part of their own development.

The training we received was a combination of live fire practice, and instruction in tactics and planning. We were also taught how to instruct our own teams in what we had learned. We spent days on live fire ranges, firing thousands of rounds at targets with photo-copies of faces attached aiming for right between the eyes. The simple and appropriate theory was that terrorists can't wear bullet resistant vests on their heads, so a double tap to the face overcame any problems.

I'm not going to describe in detail any part of the SAS base that may still be sensitive, but I can say the open range practice was supplemented by days spent in the Killing House. Targets with photocopied faces were set up in each room. The same faces were affixed to a board outside the entry to the house. The instructor would nominate which of the faces were terrorists and which were hostages and the team had thirty seconds to memorise them.

On the command 'Go, go, go!' the first operator would open the door to the house and roll in a distraction (stun) grenade. As it detonated, the team would enter the first room, identify the ter-rorists and hostages, engage the terrorists with a double tap and leave the hostages untouched. We'd move on to the next room and repeat until the entire Killing House was cleared. You didn't want to fuck up anything by shooting the wrong target. The challenge was that the terrorist and hostage photos changed each time you entered the house.

You also had to be aware at all times where your teammates were in the room and how to cover and check corners and operate safely. All this was done while the stun grenades were exploding,

Induction photo, 27 May 1977. I'm in the third row, second from the right.

Left: Detective Denis Horne. A great operator and a good mate. **Right:** Peter Kidd. He predicted that one day the Emergency Squad would be full time.

Left: Emergency Squad, Canungra training camp, 1984. **Right:** Canungra training camp, 1986. Me, Greeny, Ando and Steve (left to right).

Above: Steve Grant and me at Canungra. **Left:** With the car I demolished at the Bandiana bomb course, 1986.

Training at one of the Canungra open ranges. I'm on the left.

Left: At Bandiana in the bomb suit. I'm on the left. **Right:** HELF, our mascot for the 1986 Bandiana bomb course.

The pilot and co-pilot flying our chopper in zero visibility after take off from Amberly Air Base for Operation Borehead.

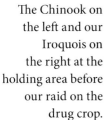

The Chinook on the left and our Iroquois on the right at the holding area before our raid on the drug crop.

Posing with the bad guys. (Left to right) Steve, me, Geoff, John and Ando.

The assault team with our RAAF crew in the crop we found on Operation Borehead.

Hamming it up for the camera.

Giblet and Ando tooled up for a shift with Rocky.

Left: Day one of the SAS instructors' course, Swanbourne, June 1987. **Right:** Entry team training at Swanbourne. I'm on the bottom rung of the ladder.

One of the SAS firing ranges. I'm on the left.

Posing with my H&K submachine gun on the SAS instructors' course.

Ready to enter the Killing House on the SAS instructors' course. I'm at the front.

Entry to the Killing House.

The entry team as a stun grenade explodes in the Killing House.

My favourite H&K MP5 submachine gun.

I'm about to give a signal to take out a target on a surveillance operation with BCI.

A Flashdance surveillance photo of Mullin's house.

The corner bedroom where Pete lay. The skirting boards show where Mullin fired at the distraction team.

The sawn-off Ruger .223 rifle used by Mullin. One of the expended bullet cases is on the floor beside the rifle.

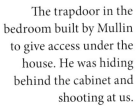

The trapdoor in the bedroom built by Mullin to give access under the house. He was hiding behind the cabinet and shooting at us.

Mullin's loaded and cocked shotgun under the coffee table.

An exterior view of the front wall of the house where our bullets were concentrated.

The front page of Brisbane's *Telegraph* says it all, as does *The Sun*'s.

The funeral of Snr Const Peter Kidd: two other officers left the force due to medical problems after the shooting.

Police Department had devoted a significant part of its budget to expanding the welfare services, but it was totally justified.

"By providing a service like that it becomes automatically cost-effective.

"If you can improve the quality of life for our people in the force, get rid of the problems that are interfering with their work, then they become more efficient."

The police force lost two other officers due to medical problems after the Paul Mullin shoot-out.

Insp Kirkpatrick said a better counselling service would help to stop the leakage from the force of good officers.

He said he was expecting a lot of people to turn-out for Const Kidd's memorial service tomorrow, at St Fabian's Catholic Church, Yeerongpilly, at 10am.

Carrying Pete's coffin.

The Sunday Mail story on Steve's recovery.

The Valour Award presentation for Operation Flashdance. I'm on the left, Steve is third from left, Peter Kidd senior and Shirley Kidd are next, and Geoff is far right.

The front page of *The Sunday Mail* after Mal and I talked down the bomber in the MLC building siege.

Just before receiving two Valour Awards from Commissioner Jim O'Sullivan, 29 July 1994.

Being presented with the Bravery Medal by Queensland governor, Leneen Forde AC in 1995.

With Mal at Government
House after being
presented with our
Bravery Medals in 1995.

On a visit to SERT in 2018. You can't take the boy out of tactical.

At the Police Academy on the thirty-year commemoration of Peter Kidd's death.

My medals.

showering sparks and light through the mostly dark rooms. We did this hundreds of times, lining up with our teams again and again.

We also learned how to breach (or force entry into) strong-holds using a number of techniques including running through safety glass. We practised vehicle assaults on targets, standing on the running boards of assault trucks while hanging on to purpose-built handholds and then smashing our way into the three-storey building that had been specifically built to be destroyed.

Venny summed it up perfectly. 'We smash all the doors and windows we can and, like magic, the next day everything's fixed and we get to do it all again. And nobody yells at us for breaking stuff. And the beer's cheap.' Life was good.

The course emphasised the importance of devising and deliv-ering a formal plan for operations to save hostages, but high-risk raids and domestic sieges also require a high degree of preparation. The knowledge I gleaned from the course was invaluable. 'Time spent in planning is never wasted time' is a phrase I remember well. Even all these years later I could still put together an emergency action plan (to take immediate action on arrival when everything is going to shit) and a deliberate option plan (a more detailed and considered plan to be deliberately implemented).

Using examples from around the world, including from the British SAS and the German counter-terrorist section GSG 9, planning training encouraged us to think innovatively and not to stick to templates for action. It also reinforced that we should use all available options including tear gas, stun grenades and special-ised breaching or method-of-entry techniques.

This was the best course I'd ever been on. As that shy kid from the country who walked through the gates in my first year of the Police Academy, I could never have imagined that one day I'd be standing with my mates on the back deck of the SAS Sergeants Mess with a beer in my hand watching the sun set over the Indian Ocean. I was surrounded by warriors and that was what it was all about for me.

At last, I was a full-time police tactical weapons operator and I couldn't see myself doing anything else. I never wanted to be a normal cop again.

CASUALTIES

Two weeks before I left for Perth, Larry finally finished undercover. His last day was a Friday and he was back in uniform on Monday. Five years of working pretty much alone, living a fake life buying drugs, lying to almost everyone and working virtually unsupervised had taken its toll. He couldn't live that way any longer and had decided to do what I'd done a few years earlier. He was back in Mobile Patrols, but he'd come to the surface way too fast and, like a scuba diver who doesn't decompress, he was suffering from a bad case of the bends. There was no reassimilation or counselling to prepare him for entry back into the world. It was simply a case of turn up and be a cop again.

Most undercovers who went back into the regular world of policing had little idea of how to be a cop again. We just had to figure it out. On my first day back at Mobiles, after finishing undercover the day before, even something as simple as using the police radio microphone seemed surreal. I understood what Larry would be going through. He'd be a stranger in a strange land.

His last job before going back in uniform had been on the Gold Coast. 'I was trying to score powder off this guy in Coolangatta,' he told me. 'He didn't trust me. We were at the Sands Hotel, and I took him out to the car. Said I had something to show him. I was blind drunk by the way, at about three in the afternoon. We got in and I took my Magnum out from under the seat, pointed it at him and cocked the hammer back. I said I wanted to see the smack, right there on the street in the middle of the day. I'm so glad to be getting out. Next time I might have pulled the trigger.'

Now that he was back in uniform and working regular shifts, we could hang out together and have a beer in a pub without worrying about who saw us. I hoped I could help him cope with the massive change.

He knew that his five years of undercover wouldn't help him get early promotion or advancement. This was still an era of promotion by seniority, and he wouldn't be considered for sergeant rank until he had done his time in uniform. It was the same for all of us, but Larry felt it the most. This was the mid-1980s, and most of police management still viewed undercover as not making a serious contribution to policing.

Coming back to the normal world was hard on a lot of fronts: the rostered shifts and night work, the accountability, dealing with the daily challenges of work in Mobile Patrols and holding your temper when some dickhead tried to bait you. But the main problem was trying to find the person you used to be before you changed into the binge-drinking, pot-smoking, risk-taking under-cover cop who no one understood unless they'd been one.

The toughest thing to accept was that the person you had once been was gone and would never come back. I'd embraced the change because undercover work had matured me and given me a more realistic view of the world. The unexpected dark result was that I was now seeking the most dangerous jobs I could be part of, and I had a growing alcohol problem. I didn't see either as an issue. Not then. I thought I was okay.

It wasn't as easy for some of the others. Undercover work kept taking its toll on my circle of friends. Having seen too much corruption John finally resigned, wanting nothing more to do with the Job. Chuck left the Job disillusioned. Spider transferred to Mt Isa with his new wife and was trying to distance himself from the drug world that had hold of him. Charlie and Zulu had both gone back to the covert world in the Bureau of Criminal Intelligence. Giblet was still in the Job, but had become a heavy pot user.

And then there was Larry. He struggled with anxiety and depression. He never spoke about it, not even to me. On the outside he was happy, always smiling and joking, apparently loving his spot back in uniform. But I could see the signs: the anger, the withdrawal from his non-police friends, the sadness when he thought no one could see him, and his need to get as high as he ever had. And, like me, his drinking had gone through the roof. We both drank for effect.

Years later I found out that he had sought help from a psychiatrist. That did him no favours. He was misdiagnosed as schizophrenic and prescribed tablets that fucked him up even more. His paranoia increased along with his anxiety. PTSD is now openly discussed and supported, but no one knew about it in the 1980s. You just coped the best way you could.

Kathleen and I were still together and planning on buying a house, so Larry moved out of the apartment they shared and into a house with other people. This change also unsettled him. He realised he needed a break to try and get his head together. His doctor gave him a long period of sick leave, and he worked on his mental and his general health. When he was ready to come back a few months later, he rang Mobiles to let the roster clerk know. A couple of days later he answered his phone at home. It was the

Personnel Branch. He was told a medical retirement had been processed and he could expect the appropriate paperwork in the mail. The Job didn't want him anymore. To make matters worse, a public servant had called him, not a senior police officer.

This was the ultimate betrayal. He hadn't been asked if he wanted to stay or go.

Larry had loved being a cop. He'd volunteered for undercover work and had put in five years, longer than anyone else. His life had changed forever but, like the rest of us, he'd been prepared to make that sacrifice for the greater good. He was shattered. The police family he'd been part of had kicked him to the gutter. No send off, no celebration of his achievements, no recognition of his sacrifice. Just a letter advising him that his medical payout would be made into his bank account and that he'd be required to return his police ID, firearm and handcuffs. So long and good luck with the rest of your life—you're of no more use to us now.

Larry used some of his payout to travel around Europe for almost a year. He tried to forget about his disappointment and his sense of betrayal and spent the time thinking about his future.

The only one who came out of undercover unscathed was Ando. He never took things too seriously. Troubles seemed to slide right over him. He'd done his time undercover, knew when to leave, and had transferred to the Task Force. He loved being a part-time Emergency Squad operator, but when the Tactical Response Group became a full-time entity he decided to transfer to a uniformed spot at Broadbeach on the Gold Coast. He and his fiancée Kerry loved the coast, and he was looking forward to opening his own taekwondo school to teach in his spare time.

I was still in Perth on the night Ando was finishing his shift as the driver of a marked police car. It was 26 June 1987. He and his colleague had been looking forward to booking off and going home. As they were driving down the Nerang Broadbeach Road, a four-wheel drive with a bull bar lost control as it came towards them at speed. It swerved across the road and smashed head on into their car.

Ando, one of my oldest and closest friends, the person who'd introduced me to undercover and taught me how to talk, how to dress and how to survive on my own in that world, was killed instantly. Just like that, he was gone, taken without reason. Kathleen broke the news to me by phone that morning. I came back on the first available flight and carried his coffin three days later.

I miss him every day.

OPERATION FLASHDANCE

5.25 am, 29 July 1987, Virginia, Brisbane
The rain had been heavy all night. It suddenly stopped and the shield of protection it had provided was gone. We were parked on St Vincents Road, which ran behind the target house at 38 Walter Street. The winter morning was pitch black, the only illumination coming from the streetlights above.

We left our Toyota Land Cruisers and moved as quietly as possible along the footpath in single file until we reached the back of a house on St Vincents Road. I gave the signal to stop, then pointed to the rear of the target house. We could see it clearly through the the yard before us.

I knew a surveillance operator was hidden somewhere in the backyard. I pressed the transmitter button on my wrist. 'Alpha 1.1 to BCI, TRG on site.'

I had no concern about my transmission being overheard. By 1987 we were using Digital Voice Protection (DVP) radios, which could not be scanned. I heard two distinct clicks in my earpiece, the universal signal for 'I understand'. The rest of the TRG team and the dog handlers waited behind us to cover the perimeter of the house.

We moved through the yard and stopped at the chain link fence separating the backyard of the target house. We stood in the darkness and watched the house. I saw the steps leading to the back door, but the house was dark and there was no movement. I had the familiar feeling in the pit of my stomach and knew my knees would soon start shaking. This was good. It meant that much-needed adrenaline was starting to flood my system. Fear is good. If you're not afraid, you get too cocky.

I gave a signal and we quietly scaled the fence, then covered the other TRG operators as they moved into position. I had planned a diversion team to set up outside the main bedroom window at the front of the house. The block sloped down towards the front, so the front of the house stood about two metres above the ground.

The nanny had explained that the rear door was missing a small pane of glass, so could possibly be opened without force. That would be perfect, an opportunity for us to slip inside and take the target peacefully. But we couldn't bet on that happening. That's what the diversion team was for. If we had to break down the door, as soon as the team heard the sound of forced entry, it would throw a ladder through the bedroom window to divert the target's attention. Seconds can make all the difference.

The two assault teams were dressed in black from head to toe, our hoods pulled up to cover our heads. Each of us carried 9 mm Heckler and Koch submachine guns in three-point slings on our chests and had 9 mm pistols with spare magazines in thigh holsters. Each man had his DVP radio affixed to his belt kit with the surveillance kit connected. We wore our white level-two vests under our blacks. They could stop pistol and shotgun fire, but nothing heavier.

I signalled Team 1 to move toward the rear of the house and Team 2 to follow. We moved in single file within touching distance of each other, exactly as we'd been trained.

As team leader, I was the last in line. Peter Kidd was the first man in the team and stopped outside the back door. Greeny was the hammer man and stood beside him. Behind Pete were Geoff, Steve and then me. Alan, Bob and Stoll (Team 2) were behind me. We each had our left hand on the shoulder of the man in front. I held eye contact with Greeny. I felt a squeeze on my shoulder, the signal that Team 2 was ready. In turn I squeezed Steve's shoulder. I saw Pete raise his right hand in a thumbs up. I signalled to Greeny to try the door. The missing pane of glass had been replaced, which meant a covert entry was out of the question. Greeny reached for the knob and then turned and shook his head. I clenched my fist and pumped it up and down. Greeny adjusted his hold on the hammer and swung it into the door lock.

A moment after the first hit, I heard glass smashing inside the house. That was the diversion team. Almost immediately I heard two gunshots from a heavy calibre weapon—heavier than ours.

Two days earlier, Monday 27 July
It was just before 8 am. I'd arrived at work and been briefed by Inspector Harry Edwards and Sergeant John Watt on the operation to arrest Paul Mullin, the most wanted man in Queensland. After the briefing, John and I went downstairs to our main office area and started the operation order for what was to be named Operation Flashdance.

John examined the intelligence we'd been provided with, and I was compiling the teams. My first choice was Steve, my best mate, colleague and former flatmate. We'd been inseparable for years and I knew him like I knew myself. I wanted him to be part of this.

Peter Kidd had also been briefed and he commenced preparing the equipment we'd need. Peter was a skilled tactical operator.

We were the same age, both focused and committed to the job. He approached me and asked to be included in the assault team.

My first instinct was to say no. Not because he wasn't capable; in fact, I knew he'd be one of the most capable members on the team. But he was married, and he and his wife had recently had a stillborn child, a tragedy that had hit them both hard. It was none of my business as a tactical operator, but as a human being and a mate I didn't want him exposed to the risk of this job. I didn't want any chance of his wife becoming a widow.

Instead of saying all this, I was the tough guy. 'Mate, I've got the teams ready to go and we need you to make sure the gear is right.'

He was disappointed, but he was a professional and took it in his stride. He went back to sorting out the equipment and I silently breathed a sigh of relief.

John and I continued to update the operation order for Mullin's arrest throughout the day. We considered several options, including intercepting him in public either while he was on foot or in traffic, but quickly dismissed those ideas as his history showed he wouldn't hesitate to shoot. We couldn't risk innocent people being caught in the crossfire.

I didn't talk about the operation when I got home, but Kathleen knew me well enough to sense that something serious was going on. I simply told her we had a job coming up and I'd be working long hours for the next couple of days.

I was still grieving over Ando, who'd been killed the month before. Kathleen had been my emotional rock in the aftermath of his death, and she probably thought my introspection was part of that grieving. That wasn't it, though. I had an ominous feeling I couldn't describe. Mullin was dangerous, but I'd been on dangerous raids before. I just didn't feel right about this one.

Tuesday, 28 July 1987

John and I arrived at the office early and kept working on the operation order. We discussed surrounding the house and calling on Mullin to come out but discarded that plan given the likelihood that he would take his partner and her two young boys hostage. His partner was also his accomplice in the armed robberies and she was to be arrested and charged as well, but our primary focus was always to save lives, regardless.

We eventually agreed that the best way to capture Mullin was to conduct a forced entry through the rear door of the house. Most of the windows were barred and the front door opened to a narrow corridor running past the master bedroom, which meant Mullin could fire through the wall at an entry team. We wrote the plan to include tear gas and distraction (or stun) grenades. The plan was for two teams to make entry through the rear door, with team 1 (Alpha 1) heading to the master bedroom and Team 2 (Alpha 2) to the rear bedroom to protect the boys. We planned to deliver tear gas via the front bedroom window and use stun grenades to temporarily blind Mullin, giving us cover to complete the arrest. It was still dangerous but, as far as an assault plan went, it was an acceptable level of risk.

Harry Edwards had flown to north Queensland the day before, but we spoke with him by phone and he was satisfied with the plan. John drove to the assistant commissioner's office to deliver the typewritten operation order and to brief him and the relevant superintendent personally.

While John was away, I had a call from a member of Alpha 1, the team that would be first through the door. He wanted to withdraw from the job. He had good reasons and I didn't blame him at all, but it meant there was a vacancy. Peter came straight to me as soon as he heard the update.

'Banksy,' he said, 'I'm the best man for the job. I'd really like to be in the team.'

I still hadn't been able to shake the sense of foreboding. If anything, it had become worse. I was determined to keep Pete out of harm's way even though I knew he'd probably hate me for it. We were the same rank, but as the team commander it was my choice alone. I looked at him steadily, but I knew I didn't have a good reason to keep him out. He was right; he was the best choice.

'Okay, mate,' I said. 'You're in. Let's get the weapons and ammo ready.' He grinned as he walked away to the armoury.

When Steve and Geoff had arrived, we signed out the four-wheel-drive troop carrier and drove to the indoor range on the top floor of CIB headquarters. Pete had brought two ammo tins containing one thousand 9 mm rounds. At the end of the practice, both tins were empty.

———

John arrived back at the depot from HQ. He was a man of few words. 'Change of plan. The bosses ruled out stun grenades and tear gas. They're worried about the kids getting hurt. And they want us to go in tomorrow morning.'

'Don't those clowns understand the risk they're putting on us?' I fumed. 'We go in with no distractions or gas and we're fucking targets. Mullin will have a home ground advantage. That's not how we operate.'

'They're the bosses, mate. We do what we can with what we've got.'

'Why tomorrow?' I asked.

'They didn't say.'

I took a breath and turned to Peter. 'Well, mate, you're in Alpha 1 with us. Let's move to plan B, once we figure out what it is.'

Within an hour, we'd updated the operation order and decided to place a diversion team outside the bedroom window, to throw their ladder in once they heard us hitting the back door with a sledgehammer, nicknamed the Ten Pound Key. Hopefully Mullin would think that's where we were coming in, giving us the precious seconds we needed to get inside. It was nowhere as effective as pumping gas inside and throwing stun grenades, but it was something.

There was one more important discussion we needed to have, and it was a team discussion about the 'order of march'; that is, who goes first, second, third and fourth through the door. Despite the risk, most operators want to be first on any job. It's the run-towards-danger mentality that prevails in the tactical world.

When I initially formed the assault team for Flashdance, Steve had wanted to be number one but I said no. He'd been number one on the previous six raids we'd conducted, and he needed a rotation from what was an incredibly stressful role. He protested, but I kept to my position. 'Yeah, mate, I know you're right,' he finally grudgingly agreed, 'but it was worth a try.'

I'd also wanted to be number one, but John had overruled me. 'Banksy, you're the team leader. The team leader is at number four. You can't be both number one and the team leader.'

Peter was all over it. 'Boys, I haven't been number one for the past few jobs. I want this one. I shot the best out of all of us today and I'm keen to do it.' That was true, he'd blitzed the practice shoot. I looked at Steve and Geoff and they both nodded. I made the decision that would haunt me for the next twenty-five years. 'Okay, Pete, you're number one.' I can still see the huge grin on his face.

All my training and experience nagged at me. I knew we should use all the tactical methods and equipment available to us, but the assistant commissioner had ordered against it. The decision, which had been made by someone with no tactical training, was out of our hands. I didn't understand why we had to go in so soon, and specifically the following day.

In a moment of downtime later that day, I made myself a coffee and glanced at the *Courier Mail*. It was the first week of the Fitzgerald Inquiry, and even that early it wasn't going well for the Queensland Police. The commissioner, Terry Lewis, had given evidence on day one and other senior police were being called during the rest of the week. I wondered how many of them had things to hide.

That evening, Pete and I took a quick break to head home, eat something and have a shower. I was back at work in under two hours.

Midnight, 29 July 1987, Alderley Police Depot
Everyone was there for the midnight briefing. Both assault teams, plus the perimeter teams, dog handlers, surveillance and detectives. John ran through the briefing before we moved to another room. A scale outline of the house's blueprint had been chalked on the concrete floor.

We spent two hours practising our entry and subsequent actions inside the house using that scale outline.

Surveillance teams had reported a possible second male in the house, most likely to be asleep in the lounge room. As Alpha 1 team leader, it would be my task to clear the lounge room on the way to Mullin in the main bedroom. Peter would be the first operator into the house, followed by Geoff and Steve then me. Alpha 2 would come in after us and head straight to the rear bedroom to protect the kids.

We double checked our personal weapons, and stripped and reassembled them. While we did radio checks, Peter laid out the white vests to be worn under our black overalls. Col Elsden, one of the detectives from the Armed Hold Up Squad, looked at the vests and at Peter. 'What would these stop, mate?' he asked. 'A .223?'

'Nope,' Peter said. 'Only pistols and shotties. A .223 would go through these like a hot knife through butter.'

'But Mullin's got a .223, boys.'

I looked at Col. 'We know, mate.'

5.30 am, 29 July, Virginia, Brisbane

Greeny smashed the hammer into the lock three or four times, but the door didn't move. The heavy calibre shots were still echoing through the house as he dropped the hammer and grabbed the door frame. Normally outside doors open inwards, but this one didn't. Peter grabbed the door frame as well. He pulled it open and broke the lock, but we'd lost valuable seconds.

Greeny stepped aside and we entered in single file, weapons up and fingers on triggers. Greeny and Alpha 2 followed right behind us.

'Police, police,' we yelled. 'Don't move.'

The house was pitch black. We triggered the mini Maglite torches attached to our weapons and made our way to the bedroom at the front of the house, the beams of light flashing on the walls. I moved to the right to clear the lounge room as more heavy calibre shots rang out. The room was empty. I turned towards the main bedroom and saw Pete push the door open and point his weapon inside. More shots sounded and then I saw him fold inwards as if he'd been struck with a hammer. He kept his weapon up and disappeared into the bedroom. More shots.

Geoff and Steve immediately followed him into the room. I took the three or four steps to get to the doorway. As I reached the door there were more shots. In the flashes of brightness Steve was propelled out of the room and onto his back, landing about a metre from the bedroom door.

When fear explodes inside of you, your sympathetic nervous system dumps natural drugs and hormones into your body to cause a high arousal state known as 'fight or flight'. One common effect is tachypsychia, when time slows to a crawl. Something that takes only seconds seems to last for minutes. Another effect is auditory exclusion when loud sounds, like gunfire, seem much quieter than they are.

In the split second after Steve flew backwards, Stoll from Alpha 2 leapt across the narrow hallway and took cover behind the bathroom door frame, firing into the bedroom as Mullin kept shooting through the open door. The sound of Stoll's shots was muted. The gunfire from the bedroom was louder, but still sounded quiet.

I took up a position on the right of the door frame and, as Stoll moved forward, I joined him in the doorway.

A naked man with a rifle pointed at us was crouching against a wall, half-hidden behind a set of drawers. Stoll and I fired until he slumped into the corner. I can still see my bullets moving through the air and hitting him in the body. I know it's impossible, but that's what I remember seeing.

We moved into the room and someone behind us turned on the light. I was in a crouch in front of a mattress on the floor, tracking my gun across the room to cover. Suddenly a woman sat up from under the doona with her hands open at chest height. In an instant my finger was on the trigger and my front sight was squarely on her forehead. The only thing that saved her from death was my training. My mind registered that both her hands were empty. I yelled at her to get her fucking hands up. She immediately threw her hands high in the air and we looked at each other.

I could hear Pete screaming in pain. My lizard brain was nagging at me to kill her, but my moral compass and my training took over again. I took my finger off the trigger but kept the foresight trained directly between her eyes. In that moment, I moved from wanting to fire at Mullin's de facto Susan Clarke to kill her with rounds to her head to sparing her life. She was no innocent bystander, quite the opposite, but she was unarmed and no threat to me.

The perimeter team was now smashing its way through the front door. John Watt came into the room, grabbed the woman and dragged her away. I applied the safety catch of my weapon with my thumb and moved to where Pete was lying crumpled on the dirty carpet.

The force of the bullets had pushed him into the rear corner of the room. He was in a foetal position, moaning at one moment and screaming in pain at the next. I went to him, removed his weapon from its sling and tore open his overalls to reveal the white vest underneath. The blood had already pumped through the vest from the four shots he'd taken to the body. I tore off the vest and saw the entry wounds. There was nothing I could do—we had no morphine to ease his pain and I had no field dressings. He'd also been hit in the right wrist. His screaming as the waves of pain hit him is a sound I will never forget. I held his hand and spoke to him. He stopped screaming. I could see he was gathering himself to speak.

'Did we get him?'

'Yes, mate, he's fucking gone.'

I looked to Stoll. He was standing over Mullin, who was on the floor on his side facing the door with the Ruger Mini-14 rifle he'd been using lying close to his hand. I looked back down at Pete to try to comfort him when suddenly I heard Steve yell. Mullin had hold of the rifle and was lifting it off the ground. Stoll spun back towards Mullin. Instinct kicked in and he shot Mullin in the head. I later learned that Mullin had been raising the rifle towards where Steve lay wounded. He obviously wanted to take one more of us with him.

I don't have much of a memory of what happened after that. Mullin was dead in the corner. I was trying to comfort Pete and at one point I raised my head to see Greeny and Geoff standing looking down at us with shock on their faces. I knew Steve had been hit but I couldn't leave Pete. The smell of cordite and blood hung in the air and I felt helpless. I couldn't go to my best mate and I couldn't do anything to help Pete. I stayed with him, trying to keep him comfortable until the ambos arrived. He was drifting in and out of consciousness. I held his left hand in mine and told him anything I could to keep his attention.

After what seemed like hours but was probably only minutes, the ambos arrived and took over. They loaded Pete and Steve onto stretchers. I was at last able to go to Steve. He was conscious but in immense pain. The bullet had hit him in the lower stomach, below the vest.

An ambo said he had enough room in his ambulance for all three, but there was no way Mullin's body was going in the same vehicle as Pete and Steve. The message delivered to the poor ambo in very low tones was unmistakable. Another ambulance was called to take Mullin's body.

'I'll see you soon, mate,' I told Pete. 'Hang in there.'

I squeezed Steve's hand as they loaded his stretcher inside. 'See you as soon as I can get there, mate.'

I don't remember travelling back to the depot. I was probably in shock. At some point I peeled off my gloves; they were covered in Pete's blood. I should have kept them as evidence but instead threw them in a bin. I went to make coffee for John, Stoll and me and brought them upstairs to the boss's office. John looked at me.

'Sit down, mate. There's no easy way to say it. Peter's gone and Steve may not live.'

I didn't sit down. Instead, I put my coffee on the desk and walked downstairs to the outside car park. I sat on the kerb. Other tactical guys came and sat with me. I don't remember much of the next hour or so but I do remember we were driven to the Homicide Squad, where we were interviewed by detectives and formal statements were taken from each of us.

I'd been awake for over twenty-four hours and was numb. The homicide detectives were sympathetic, but they had a job to do. Operation Flashdance would be investigated thoroughly and result in a coronial inquest. After taking our statements, the detectives took us to the Police Club and bought us beers. We stayed there for a couple of hours and then someone dropped me home.

I'd called Kathleen as soon as we'd arrived back at the depot. TV and radio news were reporting that two police had been shot during a raid. I wanted her to know that I was okay.

———

I didn't know it then, but that day would irrevocably change my life.

153

Kathleen was waiting with some of our close friends when I arrived home. They were wonderful in their support, but I was still in shock. I took a quick shower and went straight back to work.

Harry had flown back from north Queensland and that afternoon all the TRG operators converged in the office for a formal debriefing session. We spent the rest of the evening drinking beer at the office. No one knew how to treat us, how to look after us or how to cope with us. It wasn't anyone's fault. It was new territory for everyone.

The media coverage was immediate and national. Operation Flashdance was front-page news in the two Brisbane newspapers. It took me a couple of days to realise that the Fitzgerald Inquiry had been relegated to the inside pages. That's when I remembered the insistence from headquarters that we do the raid earlier than originally planned. A cold feeling passed through me. Surely that wasn't why Pete had died? As a distraction from the inquiry? I'll never know for sure.

When Mullin's house was searched by the CIB and forensics teams they found a loaded pump action shotgun in a bracket under the coffee table in the lounge room, cocked and positioned to fire at anyone on the other side of the table. There was a .357 Magnum revolver hidden in a PVC pipe in the yard and a police scanner beside the mattress in the bedroom. Mullin had also built a trapdoor in the bedroom that led under the house. That's where he'd been going as he was firing at us. If he'd escaped, he may well have killed more of the team who were outside on the perimeter. The back door opening outwards wasn't a coincidence either. He had changed the hinges himself specifically to slow an entry team. When the diversion team had thrown the ladder through his bedroom window, he'd leapt to his feet and fired two shots downward through the skirting board at precisely where assault team members would have been climbing the ladder. He was never going to peacefully surrender.

Steve had been shot in the lower abdomen, and the bullet had lodged a millimetre from his spine. He almost died on the operating table. Thank God, though, he pulled through. I would have been truly lost if he had died as well. Geoff and I went to see him in hospital a couple of days later. He was recovering from one of many operations to his stomach. We were in our TRG black overalls with gun belts and were tired and emotionally drained.

Steve was sleeping. We sat beside his bed. I took hold of his hand and was close to tears. He woke suddenly and looked at me. 'Mate, I'm trying to tune a couple of these nurses. If they see this, they'll think we're gay.'

We had to wait almost nine months for Steve to be well enough to give evidence at the coronial inquest. During that time, we had to tolerate the armchair experts in the media, some police and the general public telling us how the operation should have been conducted. We knew we'd done the best we could, given the limitations placed on us. Most importantly, we had saved the life of the brave bystander who'd tackled Mullin outside the Suncorp bank in Toombul Shopping Town a few weeks earlier. He and his father expressed their appreciation for our actions in the media and had contacted the commissioner's office to pass personal thanks along to us. These heartfelt thoughts went a little way to help ease the pain of losing Peter.

The massive wave of public support also helped us cope. Among the cards and letters of support was a bunch of flowers with a handwritten card from a 'grateful bank johnny'. For us, this said it all.

We also received calls and messages from other tactical teams around Australia. The blue family wrapped itself around us, which was bittersweet. That morning in Virginia had left an impact on everyone who was there, one that would not make itself known for months or even years to come.

I was to be a pallbearer at Peter's funeral, so two days after the job I got my hair cut. My hairdresser didn't know I'd been involved in Operation Flashdance and I didn't tell her.

'Hey, Keith,' she said. 'What's happened? There's a heap of grey hair here that wasn't there a month ago.' I just looked in the mirror, trying to hold back tears.

Pete was given a full police funeral with honours, and even today it still hurts to picture his grieving wife and parents. Hundreds of police marched with the hearse and members of the public lined the streets. Each state and territory police force sent representatives to pay their respects. John and Angus from the New South Wales Special Weapons and Operations Squad were among them.

On the day we laid Pete to rest, the Police Minister Bill Gunn chose instead to go to the opening of a house that was to be the prize in a home lottery. The media got hold of the story and there was hell to pay. To make amends the minister decided he'd visit Steve in hospital a few days later. But he hadn't factored in the ward matron, who was less than impressed with the swarm of media the minister had brought along to record the visit. When told by the matron that the minister wanted to express his best wishes, Steve leaned forward in his bed and grimaced. 'Tell him to piss off.'

She turned and walked towards the minister. 'He said he doesn't want to see you. He said you can piss off. And I agree with him, so piss off.' Fixed with her baleful stare, he retreated like a scolded schoolboy.

Peter was posthumously awarded the Star of Courage for an act of conspicuous courage by the Australian government and the police Valour Award by the Queensland Police Force, both honours that were richly deserved. I was proud to call him a mate.

Rest in peace, brother. Greater love hath no man than to lay down his life for his friends.

PAPAL INFALLIBILITY

During December and January of 1986 and 1987, a journalist for the *Courier Mail* published a series of revelations about the lack of action by Queensland Police in the prosecution of the vice industry. This was no news to cops; we'd all seen massage parlours openly operating and most of us knew about the illegal casinos. We also knew to stay away from them in an official capacity. Laughingly, a few years earlier the then Minister of Police Russ Hinze said he'd been on a tour of Fortitude Valley (Brisbane's well-known red-light district) and hadn't seen a single massage parlour or casino. Honest cops just let it wash over them. That was Queensland in the 1980s.

The earthquake that would shake Queensland to its foundations started with an ABC *Four Corners* program titled 'The Moonlight State' broadcast on 11 May 1987. Investigative reporter Chris Masters detailed instances of police corruption that were more entrenched than I had ever imagined. Premier Joh Bjelke-Petersen was overseas and, in a move that stunned most of Queensland, the acting premier, Bill Gunn, announced an inquiry to investigate the claims.

When I heard the news, I was convinced that the culture of secrecy and denial that had long followed Lewis and his colleagues would stymie any inquiry. I was wrong. In the end it went for almost two years.

The Fitzgerald Inquiry started peeling back the layers of the culture of the Queensland Police Force and didn't stop. The first bent cop to roll over and break the code of silence confessed on 28 August 1987, and by 16 September of that year Commissioner Terry Lewis had been implicated in corrupt activity by the direct evidence of one of his assistant commissioners.

The dominoes continued to fall with the chief bagman Jack Herbert waiting in the wings to give his evidence. The power of the inquiry meant that its budget was almost limitless and that resources and equipment were provided on a grand scale. It also had its own well-resourced witness protection section. Some of the officers recruited for that section had been transferred from the TRG and, against the strict rules of secrecy, they told me that they were travelling all over the country with their protected witnesses and being paid massive amounts in overtime and travel allowances. Many of the witnesses were corrupt police who were due to give evidence at some time over the coming two years.

I couldn't help comparing this to the way police command had treated Rocky. A genuine witness who could have brought down senior mafia figures, they put him in a cheap weatherboard house and grudgingly paid us set overtime rates. He died because he wasn't a media drawcard.

The inquiry was given coercive powers and we were told that several of its investigators had visited prisons to tout for complaints against police. Of course, prisoners always tell the truth and so their versions of the world were completely believable. They claimed they were innocent and the victims of police verbals, that evidence had been planted and so on. As far as some of the inquiry lawyers were concerned, all police were corrupt until proven otherwise. I still find the arrogance appalling.

The media was vicious in its reporting, asserting that there was a corruption problem across the whole of the Queensland Police Force. The corruption was certainly there—after all, I'd been someone who'd experienced it first hand—but it was by no means widespread. It was limited to a cohort of men who ensured they were promoted to the right places so they could fill their greedy hands with cash. The overwhelming majority of police were honest, hardworking and committed to their jobs. It affected us in many ways. I may have imagined it, but I was sure my friends outside the police were looking at me a little differently. That's what hurt.

Another consequence of the inquiry was that many police were unfairly caught up in the backwash. It was an opportunity for payback by criminals against police. The almost papal infallibility of the inquiry meant reputations could be trashed without evidence, merely on a version of truth provided to lawyers by career criminals. Once the dirt was thrown it stuck, and those wrongly tainted could kiss their careers goodbye.

In the shifting sands created by the inquiry it later became unacceptable to have an offender complain about you, whereas only a few years before it had been a badge of honour. *If you're not being complained about you're not doing your job* became *You can't be promoted because you have complaints made against you, which means you must have an integrity issue.* It's no wonder Queensland now has a crime problem that is out of control in many areas. Offenders no longer have a fear of consequences, and certainly no fear of police.

Even though the inquiry was well under way, it still wasn't easy to be honest. Trevor, a good friend of mine, had been transferred to Cairns and was a junior detective in the Cairns CIB in March 1986. He had been a police cadet the year below me in the academy and was keen to do his bit to protect the people of Queensland. He was happily married and hadn't yet become jaded.

Trevor had been given the Gaming and Prostitution portfolio, but little did he know what a poisoned chalice this would be and that the poison was Detective Superintendent Cal Farrah. Well known in the CIB network in Brisbane as being dishonest and corrupt, Farrah was a bully who treated those below him in rank with contempt. There were many stories about him, but one was particularly close to home. It concerned a friend of mine who had been instructed to drive Farrah to an exclusive shoe store in the city. My friend was told to wait while Farrah selected a pair of expensive Italian shoes. Once done, Farrah clicked his fingers for my friend to follow him out of the store. When the owner asked Farrah to pay, he was fixed with an arrogant stare. 'I am Detective Inspector Farrah and I do not fucking pay for anything.'

Farrah did this all over Brisbane, in expensive restaurants, anywhere he could throw his weight around. If any complaints were made, they were quickly addressed by a threat from Farrah that particular police attention would be paid to the establishment concerned. No wonder people believed the media reports about entrenched and widespread corruption in the police.

When he was a detective inspector Farrah was charged with perjury. It came as no surprise to anyone that he was promoted while waiting for the charges to be heard in court. After the charges were dismissed, as many against police were in those days, he was promoted again, this time to the Traffic Branch where he waived proceedings against a person who was a friend of the commissioner and other senior police. Not long after that, he was transferred to the plum position of superintendent in charge of the Far Northern region, based in Cairns. Draw your own conclusions.

Trevor took his job seriously. He paid particular attention to the illegal brothels and during visits he was frequently told, 'Your boss was just here.' That meant Farrah. Trevor and his partner, a detective sergeant, also learned that Farrah had organised a trip to beautiful Green Island, forty minutes or so from Cairns, using the police boat. The problem was that he'd taken several prostitutes with him. True to form, he paid for nothing.

Farrah's behaviour didn't stop Trevor doing his job. Targeting an illegal casino, he sent a young cop inside as an undercover observer. The undercover reported that fifty or so patrons were gambling large amounts of money. There were prostitutes and a fully stocked bar was operating. This doesn't sound like much these days, but in the 1980s it was a highly illegal operation.

As a matter of course, Trevor swore a search warrant and organised a raid on the casino. When he led the team of six detectives inside, they found twelve men of Italian descent playing cards with ten-, twenty- and fifty-cent coins. The interior was bare except for the table and chairs the men were sitting at with their cups of black coffee.

The names and addresses the card players provided to the police were obviously false. Not many people are genuinely named Mickey Mouse and Donald Duck. Farrah instructed Trevor to issue court summonses for the men anyway, saying he would arrange for them to be delivered. The following day an elderly Italian man entered the police station and asked for the summonses to be given to him. Farrah instructed that they be handed over. All the men pleaded guilty to being in an illegal casino, including Mr Mouse and Mr Duck, and the small fines issued were paid. This was not the legal process for summonses to be served, but by now Trevor knew he had to go along with Farrah's directions.

This all took place shortly after 'The Moonlight State' had been aired and Trevor quickly realised he was probably being set up as a scapegoat. When Farrah called him into his office not long after to advise him that an internal investigation into the casino raid had been conducted, he knew his gut instinct was right. Farrah handed Trevor a discipline finding that held him responsible for the incorrect service of summonses. When he protested, Farrah looked him squarely in the eye and said, 'If you don't accept this, I'll make sure things go badly for you.' Trevor understood immediately that he was the goat tethered to a stake in the middle of the forest.

Not long afterwards, a Fitzgerald Inquiry investigator and a senior lawyer flew to Cairns. Other police willingly and quickly nominated Trevor as the holder of all knowledge about illegal brothels and casinos in the far north. After all it was his portfolio, they said. 'Not my job, talk to them.' Farrah was an evil bastard, and it was best not to put your head up.

Trevor stuck to his guns and provided a full statement to the inquiry investigators. Months later he was flown to Brisbane to give evidence. It was full and frank. Farrah admitted his corruption and bribe-taking not long after. Proud of having spoken out, Trevor went back to Cairns, feeling vindicated.

But that was not the opinion held by everyone. He was called a dog. He was shut out of some police circles. He had the support of good men but was shaken by the reactions of the others.

One evening, just after he left home to start night shift, the phone rang. His wife answered and a male voice threatened her with rape. The calls continued. Both Trevor and his wife were threatened with violence, that their house would be burnt down. Trevor rightly feared for his safety and a trace was set up on his home phone. The calls were later sourced to the clubhouse of the local chapter of the Bandidos outlaw motorcycle gang. A week later, Trevor's family dog was shot and killed. This was the cowards' final message.

Farrah was gone, but Trevor had paid the price. After watching others being promoted over him, he resigned.

I know that if he had his time again, he would do things differently.

———

At first, I was buoyed by the prospect of a genuine inquiry. In the end, I was disappointed. It didn't go far enough in investigating drug networks and the involvement of corrupt police. I had thought long and hard about reporting what I knew, but in the end decided not to. This was a time when I was battling my own issues, trying to keep myself together.

I'm still convinced that Operation Flashdance was timed to draw attention away from the Inquiry. It still makes me angry. It's one thing I can't let go of.

CHANGES

While 1987 was a year that would change the Queensland Police Force forever, it would do the same to me.

A few weeks after Flashdance, Stoll and I learned that a hit had been put on us for our part in Mullin's death. We were immediately granted permission to carry our firearms off-duty, and my 9 mm semi-automatic never left my side. For almost two years I carried it everywhere I went and slept with it beside my bed. Apart from that, I didn't really change my behaviour. I'd been hyper-vigilant since my undercover days, and it was second nature to double check doors and windows and scrutinise cars in my rear-view mirror as well as vehicles parked outside my house. Sitting with my back to the wall in a pub or restaurant was second nature.

But there was no doubt that I was a changed man, and not in a positive way.

Ever since graduating from the academy, I'd been in control. I'd become physically harder and capable of holding my own in a street fight. During undercover operations I prided myself on being able to handle situations alone, hundreds of kilometres away from backup, among violent criminals and drug dealers who would have killed me if they'd learned who I really was. As a member of Queensland's elite Tactical Response Group, I was a nationally qualified close quarter battle instructor and had led countless high-risk tactical operations. I'd overcome my fear of heights to abseil down buildings, off bridges and out of helicopters. My expertise included the use of high-powered weapons and bomb disposal. Before Flashdance I truly believed that nothing the world could throw at me would crack me. Physically at least.

I didn't have trouble with dead bodies, with threats, with violence. None of those things bothered me. But what almost destroyed me was the knowledge that I had survived and Pete had not.

I still struggle to describe the anguish I felt after Flashdance. I told Kathleen everything. She was wonderful. She held me when I woke panicked from nightmares. She calmed me when I thrashed and screamed in my sleep. She loved me when I was not particularly pleasant to be with. She took care of me when I drank too much and cried. She did her best to help me, but I was lost in a chasm of grief. First Ando had been taken and, barely a month later, Pete had been murdered. Steve was eventually released from hospital, but he needed a colostomy bag for some time during his recovery. If he'd have died, I don't know how I ever would have recovered.

A few weeks after Pete's death, after the praise and recognition of his and Steve's bravery had died down, the armchair experts emerged in the media. Our actions were being criticised by people whose biggest worry in life was whether their fucking coffee was hot enough.

One front page screamed 'Mullin Pleads for Mercy'. His partner, Susan Clarke, was quoted as the source for an article that breathlessly detailed her bullshit allegations that we had deliberately taken the life of a man who was not resisting but had wanted to surrender. I have never been so angry in my life. Clarke had been Mullin's getaway driver on his two most recent robberies. I have often reflected on the fact that she had no idea how close she came to death that morning when I had my weapon pointed at her forehead. She was later charged with two accounts of armed robbery and gaoled for six years. I hope she did her time hard.

My tolerance of stupid people was over. When faced with idiots, I went from calm to white hot anger in seconds. I no longer had the patience to cope with bullshit and I lost any religious faith I may have retained from my childhood. It was all gone. I was crippled with guilt at having let Pete take part in the raid. I kept on telling myself that I should have followed my gut and not let him on the team.

About two weeks after Flashdance, a colleague of Kathleen's gifted us a trip she had won to Airlie Beach. We gratefully accepted it. I have loved the Whitsundays ever since spending a couple of months working on Hayman Island on one of the more enjoyable undercover operations. Kathleen and I spent the days relaxing by the pool and in each other's company. It did make me feel better, but it didn't take long for the sadness to fill me again.

I couldn't talk about Flashdance without tears, so I chose not to talk about it at all. I'd get to work early and throw myself into the jobs that were now increasing in frequency. It was as if Pete's murder had in some strange way encouraged the TRG to be used more and more. Perhaps the detectives now understood that if a criminal was prepared to shoot it out with a heavily armed tactical team, then nothing would stop a shoot out with lightly armed detectives.

I never spoke about it to anyone other than my trusted few, but I decided after Pete's death that I was never going to give someone a chance to drop their gun. If anyone produced a firearm and it was pointed at me or any of my team, I was going to fire as many rounds as it took to put them down. Never again was I going to put myself in the position of holding a mate's hand and lying to him that he was going to live. I wanted blood. I'm not proud of it.

I was slipping into a dark place, and I kept it to myself. I drank to numb the emotional pain. I cried often and always alone. And I started smoking pot when my mates could give it to me. It helped me sleep, and God knows I needed sleep. I would check doors and windows six or seven times before I went to bed and then I'd wake at the slightest sound, reaching over to the bedside table for the reassuring feel of the cold metal of my 9 mm. Kathleen often woke to an empty bed and she'd find me staring out the lounge room window, my pistol on the chair beside me.

Flashbacks came and went. A loud noise could trigger a memory and suddenly for a second or two I'd see Steve's body pushed backwards through the air by the force of the .223 bullet that had hit him. Other memories would come to me for no reason: a streetlight might remind me of approaching the house, or I might be at the desk at work and look down at my pistol, remembering another part of that horrible morning. The flashbacks lessened as the weeks passed but the memory of Pete dying was always just below the surface, waiting for the right moment to burst forth.

Those next weeks after coming back from Airlie Beach are a blur. I was conscious of a physical pain in the pit of my stomach, which I now know to be anxiety, and it would only go away when I drank, and I drank a lot. It became a constant cycle: start work feeling dusty from the night before, go for a run, shower, feel better, train, shoot, plan operations, go home, drink and repeat. My life was filled with constant sadness.

Then, sometime in late August, Kathleen was at a work function for the evening and I was home alone listening to 'The Green Fields of France' by the Fureys. I'd heard an SAS operator sing it in the mess one night in Swanbourne and I'd been entranced by the story of a man who chances upon the grave of a young soldier killed in the Great War. As he sits by the graveside, he wonders how the young man died. Was it quick? Was it slow? Was it glorious or was it obscene? I was drinking scotch that night and smoking one cig-arette after another, playing this song over and over. As usual my 9 mm pistol was within arm's reach.

I don't remember cocking the slide to chamber a round, but I found myself looking at the pistol in my hand with the hammer back and the safety off. I remember thinking I could make all the pain go away quickly as I turned the pistol around and pointed the barrel towards my face, opening my mouth wide and inserting it. My thumb was on the trigger and I remember a sensation of being outside my body. Just one little squeeze and I'd know what Pete and Ando knew, the answer to the ultimate mystery.

Then my mind filled with another memory. In 1982, when I'd gone back to uniform at Mobiles, my partner and I had answered a shot fired call and found a suicide victim in a house. The man had used a .303 rifle to shoot himself through the mouth. I'd been shocked by the spread and texture of the spray; by the bone and brain spatter over the wall behind the body; by the slumped body with the gun still resting against his knee; and by the sight of his skull, its top missing and only the lower half of his jaw in place.

As I sat there with the pistol in my mouth, knowing it would just take one pound of pressure on the trigger, I had an image of Kathleen coming home and finding me slumped on the couch with brain spatter over the wall behind me. In that moment of clarity, I took the barrel out of my mouth, put on the safety catch, removed the magazine and ejected the round.

I caught the round in my hand as it spun through the air and imagined the projectile smashing through my brain. I shuddered and reloaded it into the magazine. Realising what I'd almost done, I removed the slide and hid it in one place, the frame in another and the magazine in another. This was the first night for weeks that I wouldn't have my gun beside me on the bedside table.

I poured out the rest of my drink, turned off the turntable and went to bed. I waited for Kathleen to come home and pretended to be asleep when I heard her key in the front door.

When I think back on that night, I can still taste the gun oil. I didn't have a conscious desire to die; it was more about wanting to know what Ando and Pete knew. When I woke the next day, I knew I was in trouble. The problem was I didn't know what to do about it.

A week or so later Kathleen and I went to the movies. The first *Lethal Weapon* movie had been released in Australia a couple of months earlier. It focused on the battle by Mel Gibson's character to retain his sanity after the death of his wife. Partway into the film, his character is sitting alone drinking and looking at a photo of his dead wife. He takes his 9 mm pistol and inserts a round, then puts the gun in his mouth.

I tensed. I was seeing myself on the screen and it was frightening. When Mel Gibson's character removed the pistol from his mouth, unable to take the final step to oblivion, I let out a breath. I fought back tears and was filled with sadness. I knew how close I'd come. In that moment I understood the old Keith was gone forever.

———

Then a new story about Flashdance appeared in the *Courier Mail*. It was reported (correctly this time) that Peter Kidd had applied for the purchase of new ballistic vests for the TRG and that his recommendations had been refused by a police superintendent for budgetary reasons. The story was highly critical of those in charge and had clearly resulted from someone inside the group leaking the details. I wasn't the only angry one.

Within an hour of the story hitting the newsstands, the bosses at police command became consumed with trying to find out who had spoken to the press. They fiercely adhered to the old adage about not airing your dirty washing in public, particularly given the very dirty washing being thrown around daily as the Fitzgerald Inquiry continued to gather steam.

That story prompted massive media debate that quickly extended to parliament. The superintendent who had been more concerned with his budget than the safety of his people spent most of his valuable time trying to cover his arse. But once Police Minister Gunn became involved, the budget for protective vests was magically approved. Perhaps he wanted to make amends for choosing a house lottery presentation over a police funeral.

Once the budget was authorised, Harry Edwards directed me to travel to Sydney with Don, the TRG's senior sergeant, to work with the New South Wales Special Weapons and Operations Squad (SWOS) to test a variety of ballistic vests. The testing of vests provided by several companies invited to tender was to take place over two weeks. Tactical teams across Australia stood to benefit from the process as they were all using the same type of vests we had used on Flashdance.

My old SWOS friends John and Angus were familiar faces and they introduced us to the others. As was the custom, they provided beers from the office bar fridge after the working day was over and we spent a few hours drinking and talking. The legendary SWOS operator Jim Brazil, a mountain of a man with a magnificent presence who had been in the team for years and had experienced his fair share of violent encounters, looked at me steadily and asked, 'How are you going, mate?'

His sincerity moved me to tears. I couldn't speak. Unashamedly, he reached out and hugged me. I sobbed like a child, my face pressed against his chest. He said nothing but held me until I stopped. The men around us moved over and I felt other arms around my shoulders and hands on my back. 'It's alright, mate, we understand,' Jim said simply.

The toughest men in the New South Wales police force were my brothers, and without hesitation they gave me genuine support in that moment of need. Over the following two weeks, Jim and the others made sure I was never alone. I was in their company every day, including the weekends. Apart from a couple of close mates, it was support I didn't get from Queensland Police.

We spent the days at an indoor range firing high-powered weapons at the vests. Each shot brought back an image of Flashdance, of that morning at Walter Street. I got through it by picturing Mullin at the receiving end of each shot I fired. It was worth the anguish.

Following the detailed analysis by New South Wales firearms experts of the bullet-resistant properties and capabilities of each type of vest and their operational suitability such as comfort, sizing, weight and so on a final choice was made. It was the same model and make of ballistic vest that Peter Kidd had recommended. If it hadn't been for that superintendent wanting to save on his budget to ensure his next promotion, life for every one of us on Operation Flashdance might have been different.

It took over twelve months for the new vests to be manufactured. Most of us decided there was no point in wearing the useless white vests, so we conducted scores of high-risk raids without any protection. It was just luck that no one else was killed.

CONNOLLY

Redcliffe is just thirty kilometres north-east of Brisbane's central business district. It was the first European settlement in Queensland, the site of the Moreton Bay penal colony, and was later claimed as the childhood home of the Gibb brothers, who found world fame as the Bee Gees. During the 1980s its population doubled to over two hundred and fifty thousand people. That meant more banks, clubs and other places where cash was transacted. Lots of cash. That's where I came face to face with Leslie Connolly.

Connolly was a career criminal. Like quite a few criminals I met over the journey he was an intelligent man, but he preferred to live a life outside the law. He'd spent most of his life in Sydney, where he started using heroin and quickly developed a serious habit that he financed by dealing. When he shot his business partner in the face after an argument about a drug deal that had gone wrong, he was arrested and convicted of murder. He decided to appeal his conviction and was given leave to represent himself in the High Court. He won, and his conviction was quashed. That's when he sought the sunny climes of Queensland and changed his source of revenue from dealing drugs to the art of armed robbery.

This was still an era when customers queued patiently to wait their turn to be served by a bank teller. Most banks had open counters and security screens were rare. It was also the so-called Golden Age of Armed Robbery, when armed robberies were increasing in frequency and violence. Connolly was one of the few heroin-addicted armed robbers who planned and executed his holdups with precision. Most junkies didn't know the first thing about guns; they often accidentally fired their sawn-off rifles during a robbery and that was how people got hurt. But a few, like Connolly, were more calculating. That meant they were more dangerous to police because they wouldn't hesitate to take aim and shoot. Guns were a tool of the trade to them, and they knew how to use them.

That was okay with me. I was keen to be in any situation where I'd have to shoot it out. Every day I went to work hoping that I'd be called out and engage with someone who wanted a fight. I was no longer a forgiving human being. On the surface I was the same old Keith, laughing and joking, but on the inside, where only I could see, I knew I was a different man.

———

Redcliffe CIB detectives had identified Connolly as not only committing a number of lucrative holdups but as the mastermind behind them as well, including one on a racecourse and another on a turf club that had netted him over three hundred thousand dollars. On 3 November 1987 he robbed a TAB office in the suburb of Banyo.

The following day, three detectives from the Redcliffe CIB armed with photographs of Connolly taken from his criminal history file sat watching a chemist shop in their division. They knew Connolly was on a methadone program and that this chemist distributed the drug to registered addicts. It was a logical place to watch. Their patience was rewarded when a couple of hours later they saw him walk into the chemist and then leave in a Valiant sedan. They followed him and radioed VKR, the designation for the Police Operations Centre, for a number plate check.

Like Mullin and Cox, Connolly had a police scanner and heard the request for a check on his car. He retrieved his .45 calibre Smith and Wesson revolver from a bag on the passenger seat and laid it on his lap as he checked the rear-view mirror. He saw the unmarked car behind him, turned left off the main road and stopped in front of a primary school. The CIB car pulled to a stop close behind him and with that, Connolly jumped out of his car and sprinted towards the police, his large calibre revolver in hand. He pointed it at the driver's head and demanded the detectives' guns.

'Move and I'll kill all three of you,' he said, taking the keys before running back to the Valiant and driving off.

We were soon placed on standby in the event that Connolly was located. I briefed my team. When Stoll and I had shot Mullin, we used 9 mm submachine guns loaded with full metal jacketed rounds. Most of the rounds went straight through him, which is why he was able to keep firing. After Flashdance, I put away what had previously been my favourite weapon, the Heckler and Koch submachine gun. For every job after that I used either the 870 P Remington shotgun or the Armalite M16 rifle. If I shot anyone with either of those weapons, they wouldn't be left standing to shoot back. If we got the job to take Connolly, I was using the M16 with the same calibre of rounds that Mullin had fired at us.

The call came the following day. I was to take my team to an address in Redcliffe and meet Detective Sergeant Bob Munt. I knew Bob already. He was a tough man, an experienced investigator and an effective operator. He also took no crap from anyone.

Bob's information was that Connolly would be coming to an address to collect two 7.62 (.308 in civilian terms) calibre Chinese made SKS assault rifles that he had dropped there the day before after his confrontation with the three detectives. We parked nearby and snuck into the house under the cover of night.

We staged inside the house and set up fields of fire (the most effective places to shoot from) in the event Connolly resisted arrest and used a gun. I was looking at the high gate to the yard where he was expected to enter. 'What will you do if he comes in, Banksy?' Bob asked.

I didn't look around. 'If he gives me half a chance, I'll shoot him, Bob. Simple as that. If he fronts up, just make sure you're out of the way, mate. It's our job to take him.'

Bob shrugged. 'All good with me, Banksy. He's all yours.'

We spent two days and nights at the house with no result. A lot of crooks have a sixth sense, and maybe Connolly had a premonition. Possibly he drove past the house and saw something that didn't make him comfortable. I'll never know.

We went back to the office and on to other jobs, but all the time the spectre of the Fitzgerald Inquiry hung over us as it did the entire Queensland Police Force. Each day we'd wait for the latest revelation or shock news. On 27 September 1987, Commissioner Terry Lewis was stood down from his position after being adversely mentioned during the inquiry and Deputy Commissioner Ron Redmond was appointed acting commissioner. It was the end of the Lewis era, but he still had his supporters. I wasn't one. I had been too badly burnt by what I'd seen and experienced under his stewardship.

Ron Redmond was universally respected, but I knew he'd never get the top job. He'd been tainted by the past even though there was no suggestion he was involved in any corrupt activity. If you listened to the commentary coming out of the inquiry, all police were culpable for the actions of a few.

———

Christmas came and went and suddenly it was 1988. Kathleen and I had gone to a house party on New Year's Eve, and I was back at work the next day for my usual 8 am to 4 pm shift nursing a substantial hangover.

The call came towards the end of the shift. Bob Munt had information that Connolly was to meet a gun dealer on Sunday, in two days' time, to take possession of three SKS assault rifles that had been converted to machine guns. By pressing the trigger once and holding it down, all thirty rounds in the magazine would fire on fully automatic. The damage would be devastating.

My hangover was forgotten. My M16 had the same fully automatic capacity and, if I had my chance, Connolly wouldn't be touching a gun again. By then he was wanted for four armed robberies as well as the theft of the police guns and serious assault of police officers by threats to kill.

Early on the Sunday morning I travelled to the Redcliffe police station with my team, including Greeny. He'd jumped at the chance to be part of the job. We drove through Brisbane's northern suburbs towards Sandgate and finally onto the long and narrow bridge that connected Redcliffe to Brisbane. We were wearing our standard black overalls, low-slung holsters with spare magazines and carried our primary weapons. We still had no protective vests, but I knew we saw ourselves differently now. We meant business and each of us bore the memory of Flashdance. No one in my team was going to get hurt this time, I thought. Not this fucking time.

The CIB office was packed as Bob Munt gave the briefing. I liked his style; he didn't suffer fools gladly and I understood that. Bob said Connolly was travelling in a red Ford Falcon sedan with another male, aged in his thirties, believed to be a criminal associate from Sydney. They were to meet the gun dealer in the deserted car park of the Bracken Ridge Tavern, about a fifteen-minute drive from Redcliffe. Surveillance operators from the Bureau of Criminal Intelligence were part of the operation. We'd worked with them before and one of the operators, nicknamed BB, was to drive the surveillance van that my team and I would be in.

The plan was simple. We'd drive in the van to the deserted car park of the tavern and wait for Connolly, his accomplice and the gun dealer to meet. Once they were out of the car, we'd leave the van and take them out. I didn't particularly care who arrested him if he was still breathing. I was convinced, given his history, that he wouldn't go quietly. That was perfectly fine with me. I had lost compassion months ago in that house at Virginia when Pete was dying.

But as we all know, the best laid plans of mice and men often go astray. We'd been in position for a couple of hours, sitting motionless waiting for the surveillance team to alert us to Connolly's arrival, when my portable radio crackled. 'Alpha I, this is Munt.' We had provided Bob with one of our specialist radios that provided secure communications. There was no way we could be scanned.

'Go Munt, this is Alpha 1,' I whispered into my wrist mike.

'Change of location. It's now near the Eventide Retirement Home in fifteen minutes,' was the reply.

I acknowledged the call. 'Received, on our way.'

This wasn't unusual. I'd experienced changes of location and plans by the bad guys for years. Either they were never on time or they'd change their plans at the last minute. It was hard to tell whether they were clever or just unreliable, lazy bastards. I suspected the clever ones were few and far between.

BB drove the van like a true surveillance operative, treating traffic rules and red lights as minor obstacles. We made it to the area near the nursing home within ten minutes and heard the surveillance teams call the gun dealer's truck location.

'Target vehicle two is stopped just off the road about twenty metres north of Eventide. Close to the beach.'

BB drove us towards the site when another team called Connolly's car. 'Target vehicle one is approaching target vehicle two's location.'

It was one of those times when things worked in our favour. As we drove towards target vehicle two, Connolly's car suddenly appeared in front of us, having turned from a side street. Adrenaline dumped into my system and everything became crystal clear. I looked at the others and said 'Ready, ready', the signal to switch on. I looked through the front windscreen and saw the red Ford Falcon leave the road and stop about five metres away from a truck, beside which stood a solidly built bearded man.

'BB, straight on and beside the Ford, stop.' He expertly drove the van off the road as Connolly walked toward the truck. I gave the second warning order, 'Stand by, stand by', which meant safety catches off. Within a couple of seconds, Connolly had stopped. I yelled 'Go, go, go!' as we threw open the van doors. We left the van as one, weapons up and sighting on our targets. My rifle's front sight never wavered from Connolly's chest even as I became aware of two of the team moving on my left to the car where the male driver sat.

Greeny and I were laser focused on Connolly and the other man. As we approached, I yelled, 'Get your hands up, now.' Connolly threw his hands high in the air and I could see they were empty.

A wave of disappointment came over me; in that moment all I wanted was for him to have his gun. As I moved about a metre away from him, I instructed, 'On your knees, Connolly.' By now Greeny had moved behind me and had put the bearded man on the ground.

Connolly didn't move fast enough for my liking and he looked like he was considering running. Greeny was occupied with the bearded man, so as I moved closer I kicked Connolly in the upper body and knocked him onto his back. I stepped on his chest and put the barrel of my M16 to his forehead. I could feel his body trembling under me as I looked down at him. I felt no pity. This was a little bit of payback for his victims. He was doing his best to keep looking like the tough guy, but I could see the fear in his eyes. I shudder to think what he saw in mine; I was in the zone.

'Not so tough now are you, Les?' I said quietly as he lay there. 'I hope we meet again, because the next time I'm going to put one right in your fucking brain pan. Now turn over and put your hands behind your back.'

As Connolly turned over, Bob Munt appeared beside me. I looked at him and simply said, 'This time he's all yours, Bob.'

I was so focused on Connolly that I wasn't aware the other TRG operators had taken the driver of the Falcon without incident. That was how we worked; focus on your own task and trust the team to do theirs.

Back at the station for a quick debrief, one of the arresting detectives came out to find me. 'Banksy, I thought you guys would want to know this,' he said. 'The driver told us Connolly called him to come up from Sydney to give him a hand. Connolly told him what was going on and said they were going to pick up some guns. When they stopped the car, Connolly handed the old mate his gun and told him to cover him.'

'He didn't do too good a job,' I scoffed.

'I'll tell you why,' the detective laughed. 'He told us he thought about picking up the gun from the seat beside him when the van drove up to threaten the cops like Les had. But once he saw you blokes in black, he realised who you were and changed his mind. He said the word in Sydney is don't fuck around with the TRG in Queensland, they'll kill you.'

'Tell him he made the right choice,' I said. 'We would have.' I meant every word of it.

Connolly was charged with the robberies and the other offences and was sentenced to eight years' gaol, but it wasn't the last I'd hear of him.

A NEW YEAR

I hoped the success of the Connolly operation would be a portent for the rest of 1988. No one in my team had been hurt and the crook was in custody, even though I had wanted to put him away in a different manner. Things moved on.

Harry Edwards had been promoted and transferred early in the year. He was replaced by Inspector Paul Fletcher, a much younger man who had reached commissioned rank early in his career and had spent a lot of time in headquarters administration. No one really likes change, even though the world changes every day. We'd had Harry as our boss for years and were nervous about the new one, especially as he hadn't been on the road for a long time. We were worried that we'd been given a dud who knew nothing about us.

Added to this was the uncertainty about the date for the coronial inquest into Operation Flashdance. I was itching for it to start so we could tell the world what had happened and put to bed the negative press. But just as importantly, I wanted to silence the smart-arse comments some police still made about how they would have done it so much better. I'd been in the Police Club only a few weeks earlier when a half-pissed detective sneered at me. 'What happened with that job, Banksy?' he said. 'We've planned better raids on shoplifters.' A TRG mate had quickly grabbed my arm and walked me away before I had a chance to react. It's one of those facts of life: while most cops are good people, some are complete dickheads.

Harry introduced the new boss to us a couple of weeks before he left. Dressed in uniform, complete with shiny black shoes and the usual moustache, the first thing he said was, 'Men, I'm proud and honoured to be appointed to the TRG. I'm here to listen, not to tell. You blokes are the experts, not me. Call me Fletch.' True to his word, Fletch listened. He was a fantastic boss, and under him we went from strength to strength. I respected him then, and I respect him now.

Fletch was the unlikeliest administration cop I ever knew. Most had never seen an angry man, and operational police scared them. Fletch, on the other hand, supported us to the hilt. He loved a beer and knew how to get what we needed. His time in head-quarters stood him in good stead and he knew how to manoeuvre around the police bureaucracy. He was a leader; he turned up to every callout and operation, but never tried to take over. He was content to let the TRG leaders do the job, a rare trait in commis-sioned officers.

In more good news, Peter Scanlan, who had been a detective sergeant in the Break and Enter squad when I worked there as a young detective, had been promoted to senior sergeant and trans-ferred to the TRG. Scan was a great bloke. He'd gone to a private school and decided to be a cop, not a lawyer. He'd served in Cyprus as part of a United Nations police deployment. He'd also attended the prestigious Federal Bureau of Investigation course at Quantico, Virginia in the US and had been a part-time Emergency Squad member for years. All in all, things were shaping up well for 1988.

I was resigned to the fact that sadness was a part of my life. I still drank almost every day and carried my 9 mm pistol all the time, feeling naked if I didn't have it with me. But life went on. Scan actively promoted the TRG to several of his mates who were now in charge of squads in the CIB and our workload increased as a result. Not only were we doing more and more high-risk raids and improving our tactics as a result, we were also escorting high-risk prisoners from prison to their court appearances and back again. I still had anxiety before every raid and the memory of Flashdance was always just under the surface, but I kept pushing it down.

Brisbane, too, was undergoing a change of its own. It was to host the 1988 World Expo that year, altering the face of the city forever. During the six months of the expo, it was suddenly acceptable to sit at a table on the footpath and have a glass of wine with dinner. Such an idea would have been regarded with shock and horror during the Bjelke-Petersen years. Brisbane was growing up.

My personal life was also changing. I had proposed to Kathleen in March and we'd set the wedding date for July, with plans to honeymoon in the snow in Victoria.

The date for the coronial inquest was finally confirmed for May 1988. The members of the TRG were represented by Bob Mulholland QC, one of the best criminal defence barristers in the country. We knew Susan Clarke would try to allege that we'd murdered an innocent man, so we spent a lot of time preparing our defence. But as much as I was looking forward to the chance to give evidence in a court, that time spent with the legal team came at a personal cost.

I look back on that time now and know that I had regressed into a state of anxiety and near depression. My dreams came back, and my anger was again at boiling point. I worried that I wouldn't be able to get through my evidence without breaking down. In my darkest times, I found myself wishing I had shot Clarke and taken my chances with the consequences.

Clarke was represented by Shane Herbert, a criminal lawyer nicknamed Sid Vicious for the way he aggressively cross-examined police in the witness box. I'd known him for a few years after he'd defended some offenders I'd arrested, and we actually got on well enough. But I also knew he'd be acting on instructions from Clarke, and that he would be trying his best to push the coroner to commit us for trial.

As expected, Sid Vicious aggressively cross-examined each of us at length but, to his dismay, our evidence was supported by the forensic evidence. In the end, the coroner found that our actions were completely appropriate. He went further and commended all of us for our actions, specifically noting that the police gunfire had been concentrated in the area where Mullin had attempted to secrete himself when he was shooting at us.

Pete's parents and wife were at the inquest every day. It still brings a lump to my throat to think about his mother hugging us and thanking us. Bob Mulholland wiped away tears as he shook our hands. Shane Herbert and his client left the court without a backwards look.

The news was swiftly passed to those who mattered. Steve and Greeny were on the range in Swanbourne attending the SAS course when an Army captain stopped their training to announce the coroner's findings. We knew we had done everything correctly in using lethal force, but it was still a relief to hear the coroner say our actions had been justified.

Kathleen and I were married in July at a church in Clayfield surrounded by family and friends. Two motorcycle cops who were part-time members of the TRG escorted our wedding cars. Steve was my best man. We were in love and, like all newlyweds, we looked forward to a bright future.

———

The next day we flew to Melbourne. While Kathleen had lunch with an old friend, I arranged to meet Jim Venn from the Special Operations Group at the Victoria Police Club, where we drank beer like it was a race. At some point in the afternoon, Venny brought someone to the table to meet me. 'You've both got something in common,' he said. 'Mark's been shot, and you've shot somebody.' That someone was Mark Wylie.

In 1986, a bomb placed in a car parked outside the Russell Street police headquarters in Melbourne by career criminals Craig Minogue, Stan Taylor and Peter Reed exploded. The cowardly attack killed a 21-year-old constable, Angela Taylor, and injured twenty-two others. A month later, Mark and his team raided Reed's home in Kallista, a small town just to the east of Melbourne. As Mark approached a bedroom, Reed shot him through a door with a .45 calibre pistol. The bullet hit him in the side, went straight through his body and was caught in the lining of his parka. Mark wasn't wearing a vest (in a stark reminder of Flashdance, there weren't enough to go around). Reed was immediately shot and wounded by another detective. As Mark unzipped his parka, the bullet fell to the floor. He felt himself passing out, but just before he collapsed he told one of his colleagues to mark the spot where the bullet had fallen for crime scene analysis. That's courage.

Mark had survived being shot but he was left with the dark spectre of PTSD, something that we shared but neither of us understood at the time. At one point I asked how he was doing and he just shrugged, but I knew he'd also been changed. He told me that when he was lying in hospital he'd decided there was more to life, so he'd enrolled in a business degree part time. We made no plans to stay in touch. He was just another good bloke I'd met along the way. Little did I know that one day, years into the future, he would become influential in my life.

THE ABYSS

Kathleen and I returned to Brisbane and settled into married life and I settled back into tactical work. I tried to disguise my growing emotional turmoil with my usual banter and humour, but I knew it was a sham. I only felt fulfilled when we were on a job, regardless of how big or small it was. I loved kitting up with my team and going on every job I could.

There had been a marked increase in the use of firearms against police over the previous few years and it was becoming even more frequent. When I'd first joined as a young cadet in 1975 it was common for police to be injured on duty but that was generally because they'd been heavily outnumbered and bashed by groups of cowards. By the late 1980s, however, armed robberies were increasing, up to an average of one a day, and it had become more common for crims to fire shots at cops as they tried to escape arrest. As a consequence, we were now doing high-risk jobs, from prisoner escorts to sitting near banks or building societies waiting for armed robbers to strike, almost daily. I loved it. I pushed my sadness downwards and knew it was being replaced with cold-blooded ruthlessness.

I am convinced everyone is capable of extreme violence, but I am equally convinced most of us never tap into that dark side or that we are ever aware that it lurks somewhere in us. My problem was that I was not only aware of it, I was happy it was announcing its presence. I wasn't just changing a little; I was on the verge of jumping straight into the abyss. Not long after our honeymoon I was jolted by a sudden realisation of where I was heading.

On 1 August 1988, a twenty-eight-year-old man took his mother hostage in a first-floor unit in the suburb of Runaway Bay on the Gold Coast. When police arrived, he opened fire on them with a rifle and kept firing shots at any visible police. Over the course of the next two hours, he also threw two Molotov cocktails at police cars, successfully setting fire to one of them.

We were called out to respond and met at the TRG office in Alderley. The Fitzgerald Inquiry was still siphoning off a great deal of overtime and resources to protect bent cops who were rolling over on each other, so overtime for the rest of the police force was limited. This meant only four of us from a tactical team were authorised to attend the siege. Scan, our senior sergeant, and two negotiators were also on their way. To put this in perspective, a domestic siege would normally have a response of at least twenty TRG operators; here shots had been fired and a police car set alight, and yet we were only permitted a total of seven men.

We met at our office, signed out the keys for the heavy equipment truck and headed to the Coast with sirens and lights activated, driving as quickly as we could. By the time we reached Runaway Bay, a cordon of general uniformed police was in place. Fletch and Scan met us at a holding area set up in the ground floor unit immediately below the gunman. The negotiators were already on site and had made telephone contact with the man, trying unsuccessfully to talk him out.

Our standard operating procedures kicked in and we quickly agreed on an Emergency Action (EA) plan. It was simple: if it went to shit and it looked like the gunman was about to shoot his hostage we would smash down the door and go in. Sometimes that's all an EA involved.

I wasn't the assault team leader on this operation; that fell to Bob and he briefed Scan, who had started preparing the Deliberate Option (DO) plan. We were in a staging area on the set of stairs leading to the first floor and only metres from the front door of the target unit when suddenly, and without warning, the gunman let loose a volley of shots. I turned to my teammate and said, 'If I get a chance, I'm going to kill this bloke.' It was as cold as that.

Scan called the four of us back to the ground-floor unit from where he and the negotiators were operating. Part of our DO was to use a gas gun (a single-barrel weapon that resembles a huge flare gun) to deliver enough tear gas into the unit from an adjoining first-floor balcony to force the gunman to surrender. The plan required me to climb up to the adjoining balcony, fire the gas canister through the kitchen window and follow that up with a hand-held gas grenade. Once I'd delivered the gas, I needed to descend from the balcony, make my way back through the ground-floor unit to the stairs and then join the assault team. Without resources, you do what you can.

Away from the negotiators who were doing their best to talk the gunman out, Scan quietly explained the situation. 'There's a bed-bound quadriplegic in the unit across the street from the hostage taker. That last volley of shots was aimed at the man's bedroom. The hostage taker told the negotiators he's convinced that a red light he can see in the bedroom is a cop having a cigarette. The red light is the intercom this poor bloke uses. The negotiators can't convince him otherwise. He's going to keep shooting at the unit and the quadriplegic can't be moved. I'm giving authority to implement the DO.'

I loaded the gas gun and scaled the building to the balcony. Once there, I radioed Bob. 'Alpha three in position. Stand by for gas.' I heard the two clicks in my earpiece acknowledging my transmission. I was protected by the dark but could clearly see the kitchen window in the target unit. I could feel my blood pumping, and the familiar surge of adrenaline was flooding my system. I welcomed the rush and knew from experience that this ensured my focus was at maximum. I aimed the gun and fired a large canister, which smashed its way through the flyscreen covering the window. I dropped the gas gun, immediately picked up the gas cannister and pulled the retaining pin. I could hear the gunman yelling something from the unit as I aimed and threw the cannister through the gap in the flywire. It arced through the air and the retaining pin flew away, activating the gas charge. With that, I vaulted over the balcony, hanging by my hands for a second to allow a gentle drop to the ground. I ran to the ground unit, picked up my shotgun from where I had left it beside Scan and bolted up the stairs to join the team just as the entry man smashed the door with a sledgehammer.

The gunman ignored the yells of 'Police, don't move' and made the mistake of raising his rifle towards us as we entered. He was shot once in the chest and collapsed. Unlike in the movies, people don't fly backwards in the air when a bullet hits them. He crumpled forward, dropped the rifle and fell face down to the floor.

In what seemed like an instant, the hostage was removed and passed down the stairs to uniformed police, the rifle was taken from the gunman's reach and secured and the unit was cleared. Ambulance officers, who had been on standby, quickly entered and removed the wounded gunman.

The familiar smell of cordite and blood hung in the air as the clouds of tear gas were dispersed by the breeze coming through the open balcony door. As we regrouped before we left the unit, one of my TRG mates nudged my arm. 'Banksy,' he said, his voice muffled by his gas mask. 'Let's get the fuck out before that thing realises we're here and takes us all on.' He pointed to the television set, where a cat sat quietly licking its paws and cleaning its face. 'That's the toughest cat I've ever seen.'

He had a point. Shots fired, yelling and screaming, tear gas, sledgehammer, more shots, more yelling . . . and the cat just sat calmly ignoring us. It's one of the funniest things I've ever seen.

A few hours later the team was at my house in Brisbane drinking at my home bar. We stayed up all night and went to the office that morning, still pissed and smelling of tear gas.

———

When we arrived at the office, Fletch shook our hands for a job well done. And then he said, 'Alright you lot, go home and shower. You smell like a combination of the tear gas hut and a brewery. Inspector Jones from Personnel is coming to see you at 10.30 today. Probably a good idea to make yourselves a bit more presentable. Don't drive, for fuck's sake. I'll get a couple of the boys to take you home and bring you back.'

When the inspector arrived a couple of hours later, he told us that he had arranged for the Government Medical Officer (GMO) to meet each of us that afternoon to check on our welfare. After Pete was killed, it had apparently been decreed the GMO was to assess personnel involved in major incidents. I remember thinking what a major step forward this was and that perhaps top brass was thinking about welfare differently. I knew I was standing too close to the edge and that things were getting worse. Maybe this was a chance for me to be open about the nightmares, my struggles, my emotional numbness and my thoughts that I was losing my humanity.

The interview took approximately two minutes. 'Banks?' the GMO asked, looking at his list.

'Yes doc, Senior Constable Keith Banks.'

'You look alright,' he said, looking up at me. 'How are you feeling?'

I wasn't going to commit to anything. 'Okay.'

The GMO scribbled something on his paper and said, 'Good, see you in two weeks. Can you send in the next one?'

At least somebody had asked us how we were, I suppose. It was my fault I couldn't be honest, but I didn't know what difference it would have made. All I know is that I didn't want to be taken away from the group, my mates and the action.

———

I ran into Inspector Jones a few days later at headquarters. I could see he was genuine when he asked how things were. I didn't have the heart to tell him that the new welfare interview process with the GMO was a profound waste of time, that I could feel the darkness taking me over day by day. Instead, all I said was: 'I'm pretty good, sir. Thanks for your help.' He smiled and walked off. He was a nice guy, just way out of his depth with us.

I knew then that I had been looking into the abyss for too long; I was turning into something I'd never wanted to become.

THE BOGGO ROAD FUN RUN

The problem with putting crooks in prison is that they have a lot of spare time to think. This means they have lots of time to devise innovative ways to either escape custody or attack other inmates. I've seen the results of some horrific assaults, and attempted murder and murder are all too common in prison.

Boggo Road Gaol was Brisbane's main prison for over one hundred years; it opened in 1883 and closed in 1992. In the middle of Dutton Park, now a trendy inner-city suburb with coffee shops and its share of hipsters, its entrance faced Annerley Road and was marked by two imposing steel gates overlooked by guard towers with armed prison officers. I'd been in there a few times as a young cop to collect prisoners and every time those huge steel gates clanged shut behind me, I gave thanks I was an honest man.

An old-fashioned prison with old-fashioned ideas of prisoner control, the consequence of prisoner misbehaviour at Boggo Road was a bashing and/or time in solitary confinement in the primitive punishment cells, located under A Wing. These cells had no running water, ventilation, natural light or sewerage and contained just a water jug, a toilet tub and a fibre mat.

The prison housed some of the most violent crooks in Queensland's history including James Finch and John Stuart, who were sentenced to life for the murder of fifteen young nightclubbers in the Whiskey Au Go Go arson attack in 1973. Arthur James Murdock, a notorious and violent rapist, was locked in a small cage for years to keep him away from other prisoners and prison staff. It was rumoured that every new prisoner was given a reception bashing to let them know the prison officers were in charge, not them. It's hard to imagine that happening today with the focus on prisoner rights and rehabilitation, but in the 1980s Boggo Road wasn't the only prison rumoured to use these methods.

———

On a sunny afternoon on Saturday 11 March 1989, a laundry van finishing its regular rounds inside the prison drove slowly towards the gates. Prisoners were jogging or walking around the Number 1 Division oval just inside the entrance. There was nothing out of the ordinary, but on this day approximately thirty prisoners ran towards the gates before they closed behind the van. They had planned to hijack the van. Nine prisoners managed to get through the inner gates but were stopped when the outer doors would not open. One became trapped when his leg was caught in the closing gates. (The outer doors would not function unless the inner gates were completely shut.)

Two of the prisoners were armed with 'guns' that had been smuggled inside; one was a replica and the other a homemade 'zip' gun. They grabbed a prison officer and fired a shot in the air and demanded that he unlock a side door beside the main gates. He did just that, and the eight prisoners ran down the driveway past the visitors' area laughing as they went. (The escape subsequently became known as the Boggo Road Fun Run.)

A guard in the tower fired two shots at the prisoners, but he missed. Others gave chase. One of the prisoners hijacked a taxi but was caught as he tried to drive away. He'd been inside for so long that he'd forgotten how to make the car move. A second was captured in the Brisbane suburb of Logan later that day. Five were caught within a few weeks. Only one really got away, my old friend Les Connolly.

Connolly left Queensland as quickly as he could and made his way to Tasmania. He remained on the run until July, when he was captured in Hobart without resistance. I like to think he remembered our chat after he'd been captured when he held up three detectives and stole their handguns. I'd had him at the end of my M16 rifle telling him that if I saw him again, I'd shoot him in the head when he'd realised that discretion was the better part of valour. Perhaps he thought that as much as he enjoyed meeting me in Redcliffe, it was probably best our paths didn't cross again. Or maybe he just didn't like the Brisbane winter.

TIME TO GO

The days blended one into the other. Planned jobs, callouts, bomb responses, more jobs and then drinks and home. Kathleen was being promoted into more senior roles in her advertising career and, in those days of wine and roses, she often had long lunches with clients. The result was we didn't see a whole lot of each other and, to be brutally honest, I probably wasn't great company anyway.

The change in my personality was starting to worry me. I had extreme anger and, where I once took a conciliatory approach to many things, I was now confrontational. More importantly, I was losing any sense of emotional attachment to people I loved and would often spend time alone with my thoughts. I worried that I was going crazy, but I didn't dare ask anyone what they thought of my state of mind.

At one stage in late 1988 an additional senior sergeant was transferred to the TRG. Ron had been a negotiator with the group for years and the rumour was he had been sent to keep us in line, because we had shot more people in eighteen months than in the history of both the Emergency Squad and the TRG. I don't know if that was true, but the cops are just as gossipy as anyone else and they love a good conspiracy.

If the rumour was true, it was probably the sensible thing to do because I am damn sure I wasn't the only one wanting blood after Pete's murder. But at the time I thought it was fucking insulting and I railed against the change. My problem was that I was the outspoken one, so my head was well and truly above the parapet. Scan took me aside a few times and was the only one to ask if I was okay. Of course I lied and said I was fine, but I knew I was fast losing control. I had to do something.

Sitting outside the doctor's surgery waiting for my appointment was painful. I didn't know what to say: *Doc, I can't sleep, I want to hurt people, I feel so much sadness, I need a break, can you help me?* These thoughts all ran through my mind as I waited for the receptionist to tell me it was my turn.

The longer I waited the more anxious I became. *I can't say that. He'll think I'm fucking mad. Maybe just tell him I can't sleep and ask for a couple of days off. Yep, that should do it.* The receptionist called my name and I walked through the door. As it closed behind me, the doctor said, 'Hello, Keith,' and asked, 'What can I do for you?'

I burst into tears and couldn't stop.

I was given a sick leave certificate for two weeks. When I could pull myself together, I thanked the doctor and drove home. I called the office and told the administration clerk I was on sick leave. Three or four days later, my pager buzzed with a message to call Scan. I rang him at the office.

After the usual hello, he hesitated for a couple of seconds. 'Sorry, Banksy,' he said, 'but the superintendent found out you're on sick leave and he's instructed me to ask you why.'

My anger leapt sky high in a microsecond. I had a confidential medical certificate stating a 'medical condition'. It was completely inappropriate for the question to be asked. This superintendent had the emotional intelligence of a brick and the arrogance to think the rules didn't apply to him. But even through my anger, I had enough presence of mind to know that Scan was on my side.

I controlled my voice and replied, 'Just tell him I've got a sexually transmitted disease that will possibly infect the whole office and I need to be quarantined.'

There was silence, then a chuckle. 'How about we tell him you've got a bout of flu? And don't come back here and tell anyone you're infected; they'd probably believe it. Get some rest.' He was a good man and a great boss.

I knew my dark side was in danger of taking me over and it was only a matter of time before I lost control. Someone close to me told me that I'd lost the smile from my eyes and I didn't doubt her for a minute. I could see what I was becoming. I had to find a way to stop it before it was too late.

When I came back to work, that choice was made for me. Ron, the senior sergeant, put it simply. 'I think your time is done here; you should think about a transfer back to Mobile Patrols.'

I understand now that he could see how much I was suffering and that he wanted to help me, but he could have phrased it better. The only thing I heard from that conversation was that all my work and sacrifice counted for nothing. I wasn't wanted anymore. That hurt me deeply.

I blinked back tears, kept my silence and walked out of his office and straight into Scan's. I told him I'd been told to transfer, but I wasn't going back to uniform. If I had to leave, there was only one place I wanted to go.

My transfer to the Bureau of Criminal Intelligence (BCI) was announced in the transfer list about six weeks later and was to take effect at the end of July 1989.

But the universe wouldn't let me leave the TRG without one last thing to remember it by.

———

On 29 June 1989, a woman and her new partner arrived at a block of units in Wynnum West to retrieve some property as part of a separation. An argument started between the woman and her former partner and he stabbed her several times in the chest, back and arms. The woman and her new partner ran downstairs and escaped through the front door, but as they did the man shot at them from the first floor of the unit with a heavy calibre .303 rifle and one of the shots hit the new partner in the back. They managed to climb into their car and drive to a doctor's surgery nearby. The woman and the gunman had a two-year-old daughter. A neighbour picked her up from just inside the door and ran with her towards safety. The gunman fired again and the shot passed through the neighbour, killing his daughter who was cradled in the woman's arms.

Constable Brett Handran and Senior Constable Steve Clarey, both plain-clothes officers with the Juvenile Aid Bureau, were in the vicinity and responded to the call from Police Operations for any units to attend. They sped to the scene, arriving around the same time as uniformed police.

Brett got out of the car first and took about four steps to where the other police cars had stopped. The gunman suddenly appeared again on the first floor and shot Brett in the back as he was turning to Steve, who was just stepping out of the passenger side of their unmarked car. The second shot grazed Steve's head as he took cover behind the door.

By chance, we had been training nearby and were despatched immediately. We made our staging area in a school adjacent to the rear of the units and, as per protocol, I directed snipers to cover entry and exit points and provide updates on movement inside the target unit. I was briefing the team on the Emergency Action plan when we were told Brett had died on the way to hospital. He was twenty-three years old.

There is no best way to describe the emotions police feel when one of their own is killed. Anger, disbelief and sorrow are under-pinned by the need for cold and total revenge. I looked at each one of my assault team. Nothing needed to be said aloud. We all knew the risks involved by going in; we also all knew that if this gunman gave us any reason at all, he would not be walking out.

We were given authority to enter and approached the gunman's unit from the rear side of the unit block. Access to the ground floor of his unit was via a sliding glass door that led into the unit's kitchen. By good fortune, this door was unlocked and we quietly opened it to find an infant crawling around on the kitchen floor. Two members of the team gathered him up and took him outside.

We silently cleared the kitchen area and carefully went up a flight of stairs. As we got to the top of the stairs, we found the gunman lying on his back with most of his head missing. The coward had taken the easy way out. The .303 rifle lay beside him.

I moved past his body with the others to clear the rest of the rooms. My boots crunched on bits of skull scattered on the floor with his brain matter. My only thought was *Oh great, now I'll have to find a hose somewhere to clean that off.*

There was a campaign for Reach toothbrushes on TV at the time that featured a cartoon character whose head opened hori-zontally to allow him to clean his back teeth. 'You can either get a

207

flip-top head,' it said, 'or a Reach toothbrush.' As we walked through the remains of this man's head, Steve Grant, who'd recovered from his gunshot wound and was well and truly back in the game, looked at me and announced, 'Well, this cunt won't need a Reach toothbrush, he's already got the flip-top head.'

Cop humour. Black as night.

Later that afternoon, we were directed to attend the Wynnum Police Station. The higher ups were deeply saddened by the death of our brother officer and wanted to support us we were told. But when the assistant commissioner who had called us to the meeting began his address, it became clear that he couldn't remember Brett's name and had to be prompted by his staff officer. I didn't care about the fear I felt going into the unit or walking through the gunman's brain matter, but the fact that the assistant commissioner couldn't remember a murdered officer's name on the day he'd been killed made me very, very angry. It still does.

Four days later, on the day of Brett's funeral, the Fitzgerald Inquiry report was released. It couldn't be delayed, even by a single day, out of respect for a murdered young officer. Brett's grieving family and his colleagues were pushed to the side by a media breathlessly extolling the virtues of Fitzgerald and his epistle from on high.

A month later, I was in the BCI and hoping for a change. I wanted to find the old Keith and bring him back but suspected that was impossible.

BELOW THE SURFACE

The Bureau of Criminal Intelligence (BCI) was a secretive unit that gathered and analysed intelligence on criminal organisations, including outlaw motorcycle gangs and Italian organised crime. It also provided covert surveillance to assist investigations throughout the state. That meant teams were often sent away.

On my first day I was assigned to a surveillance team to learn the trade. On my second day I was part of a team doing surveillance on an armed robbery suspect who we then detained at gunpoint as he left a shopping centre. I loved the buzz of being able to stroll up to his car and suddenly point a pistol at his head without him seeing it coming. So much for moving away from my dark side.

I quickly learned that surveillance is nowhere near as easy as it looks in the movies and on TV. Sitting in a hot, windowless van with no air conditioning for hours on end in Brisbane humidity is not fun, although it is an excellent way to shed a couple of kilos. I also learned to use cameras, listening devices (we had the legal right under warrant to place listening devices inside houses and apartments), tracking devices and other surveillance equipment and to follow targets in cars and on foot. I enjoyed the solitude and the relative freedom of the BCI. And I could grow my hair, put my earring in and not look like a cop.

I was soon given my own surveillance team and spent a lot of time away from Brisbane. As much as I loved Kathleen, I also loved being free of domestic responsibilities. The culture of doing jobs away meant we ended each day with dinner and drinks, often not finishing until after midnight. We shared motel rooms so we could save most of our travel allowance to spend on drinks. Without realising it I was self-medicating. It was a perfect way to rationalise my alcohol reliance.

'Work hard and play hard' was the motto. Any cop in Australia would tell you that that's how things were back then. I was always waiting for the next job out of town. When the weather turned a little colder, I'd lobby mates in the drug squad for surveillance in north Queensland. This went on for a couple of years. I'm not proud of those days.Kathleen did her best to support me and love me, but I was in an emotionally downward spiral. I sought validation from others and convinced myself that she didn't understand me. I treated our marriage badly. I was emotionally unavailable and withdrew, not just from her but from almost everyone. I felt isolated from the world and I know I broke her heart, something I will always regret.

One morning I woke up, said goodbye and left home without a plan or anywhere to go. I was overwhelmed with sadness and I wanted to dwell in that alone. I spent a couple of nights sleeping in my office until a colleague offered me a spare room while I looked for somewhere to live. I was living a cliché—burnt-out cop, separated from his wife and living for the Job.

Kathleen had been the centre of my life before Flashdance, but within a short couple of years I found myself in a place I never imagined I'd be. I was the guy to catch up with if you wanted a big night out, any night of the week. I was the first person at the bar and the last to leave.

I must have told the Flashdance story dozens of times, often to the same people, and it always made me cry. I was trying to express something I didn't have the words for, and they'd listened because they didn't know what else to do.

Police drank for hours most nights in Brisbane, but the golden rule was that you turned up to work the next day. You would never let the team down by taking a sickie. Even before Flashdance, I remember leaving nightclubs like Sybil's or Rosie's early in the morning and rolling in to work a couple of hours later to execute a search warrant. It wasn't just me—a lot of young cops operated on a few hours' sleep after a late night. Even if you were a bit late, your mates would cover for you.

One morning I was at the office when my desk phone rang. I answered in the usual way, 'Banks.'

'Banksy, I don't know where I am,' a voice whispered in reply. 'I'm at some girl's place and she's still asleep.'

'Go outside, look at the nearest cross street for a sign and page me from a phone box. I'll come and get you,' was my sage advice.

In those days being able to drink was a sign of toughness. Being known as someone who 'liked a drink' was almost a badge of honour. The Transcontinental Hotel was conveniently across the road from police headquarters, and it was not unusual for some of us and on-duty detectives to be in there most nights. This made it easy for me to continue my love affair with alcohol because it wasn't anything out of the ordinary, no matter where you were stationed.

In the early 1990s a young cop nicknamed Irish who'd been in one of my undercover circles was working as a plain-clothes constable on the Gold Coast. Heading home after a day shift spent drinking, he stopped at a bottle shop to buy some rum. As he was leaving, he tripped and fell over and his police-issue revolver slipped out of his waistband, skidding across the footpath. He got to his feet, retrieved his gun and climbed back in his car. His next memory was waking up in the police station. He'd fallen asleep in his car and bystanders had called the police.

Just as they'd done with Larry, Irish was quietly paid out as medically unfit. He never worked again. It was easier to get rid of the problems than to admit liability and help.

When we were undercover, we felt invincible. Our whole lives were ahead of us. We could not have imagined how irreparably damaged so many of us would end up being. I remember how sad I felt when I heard about Irish. Pissed, staggering around with a gun in his belt and completely alone. What happened to him was a direct consequence of being undercover. We smoked pot and carried guns. We led reckless lives without supervision, and when we were of no more use we were sent back to uniform. There was no transition, no support. No wonder a lot of young men were destroyed by what they saw as a noble cause.

REFORMS

The Queensland government was reeling from two years of the Fitzgerald Inquiry. Political, police and criminal scalps had all been claimed, including that of the police commissioner Terry Lewis. There were certainly no Queensland candidates to replace him so, on 1 November 1989, Noel Newnham, an assistant commissioner from Victoria Police, was announced as the new Queensland Police Commissioner. The decision seemed to be primarily about the optics.

Newnham arrived in Brisbane by police plane and stepped onto the tarmac wearing his full Victoria Police uniform, complete with cap and his full-sized national medal dangling from his chest. The premier and police minister were there to greet the much-touted future saviour of the Queensland Police and to take advantage of the media opportunity. As they walked towards their new commissioner, Newnham stood to attention and threw his snappiest salute, scaring the crap out of the police minister, who probably knew that the salute is reserved for others in uniform and was certainly not to be used for a politician.

This was not the leader I expected from a force as universally respected as Victoria Police. A few days later my mate Jim Venn from Victoria's Special Operations Group called to wish us all luck with the new boss. He said we'd need it.

Commissioner Newnham introduced what I'm sure he saw as valuable reforms, including directing that all unmarked police cars be fitted with the large adhesive insignia on both front panels to show the public that there were many more police on the road than they realised. This was probably a good idea in the classroom, but totally unrealistic when it came to sitting in a car park waiting for armed robbers to hold up a bank. The insignias must have been magnetically attracted to cement, because whenever I drove into the car park under headquarters they seemed to self-adhere to the sides of the cement pylons supporting the building in the strangest fashion.

Another 'reform' was to change the name of the Queensland Police Force to the Queensland Police Service. Announced in 1990, this was about image over substance and was met just as favourably by serving police as the commissioner's first induction parade at the academy when he told the new recruits that they, like the protagonists in *Star Wars*, were the new breed fighting against the dark force of the old police. Anyone who was a senior constable or above was either corrupt (and hadn't been caught) or they knew about corruption and condoned it, the recruits were told.

Commissioner Newnham didn't have his two-year contract renewed and was replaced by Jim O'Sullivan, a Queensland cop who had served many years as a detective. O'Sullivan had headed the Fitzgerald Inquiry's investigation area and had been instrumental in the arrest and prosecution of many corrupt police.

—

Fitzgerald had been critical that so few police had tertiary qualifications, so as part of the government's complete acceptance of all things from Fitzgerald police were strongly encouraged to undertake tertiary study. A Bachelor of Justice Studies degree was especially designed and introduced. To make the degree more appealing, attendance at classes was permitted during rostered shifts.

The unofficial line was that if you ever wanted to be promoted, you should at least be enrolled in the degree and working on it. I personally didn't see it as a bad thing; I thought a lot of cops could benefit from studying and I was looking forward to it. I enrolled and started attending classes, including one on intelligence gathering and analysis that was perfect for me. The tutorials were given by a mix of lecturers who had differing views on police. My Social Justice tutor was not a fan of police or government. I didn't like her attitude, but what I learned from her classes was to debate with fact, not emotion. This was challenging, given that I was quick to anger, but I persevered. I'm pretty sure I won her over when I produced an assignment arguing for the legalisation of drugs, an interesting point of view from a cop.

The university library was open at all hours. I enjoyed the solitude and being in the library was like visiting an old friend. Libraries had been a refuge for me during my challenging childhood, providing a place of peace away from the rage of my stepfather.

Researching an assignment one weekend, I took the opportunity to read some US police journals. I'd read a lot of articles regarding officer safety and tactics over my police career, but as I was browsing the journals in the library I found an article about common post-shooting reactions. I scanned the page and saw a list.

Anger
Intrusive thoughts
Loss of emotion
Rage

Alcohol or drug abuse
Depression and anxiety

Suddenly I realised I wasn't alone.

I picked up the journal and photocopied the article. Then I gathered my things and went outside to sit in the shade under a large fig tree. I read the article in detail. The sense of relief was massive. It wasn't just me. It didn't have a name yet, but this was happening to other cops as well.

I don't know how long I sat there, but after I finally went home I cut out the list and put it in my wallet. I would keep it there for years and look at it to remind myself that I wasn't crazy. The problem was I didn't know what to do about it.

WINGCLIPPING

Not long after getting my own team to manage, I was given the added responsibility of the Wingclipping desk. This was a national project with its origins in the Australian Bureau of Criminal Intelligence (ABCI) in Canberra. The ABCI provided intelligence and assistance for all national intelligence projects involving organised crime and each state Bureau of Criminal Intelligence (BCI) managed the projects at a state level, cooperating across borders to gain intelligence to assist with criminal investigations. Wingclipping was one of those projects. In one of those 'what a small world' experiences, the Wingclipping project had previously been managed by Zulu, my old friend from the undercover days and the Emergency Squad.

I'd always maintained that outlaw motorcycle gangs (OMGs) were more than a bunch of blokes riding around because they liked motorbikes, but the BCI opened my eyes to what they really were. I quickly learned that many OMGs are highly organised criminal gangs with international connections to facilitate their drug dealing, prostitution and extortion rackets as well as other criminal enterprises. I also learned that the Canadian law enforcement authorities listed OMGs as their number one criminal threat, with the Mafia as number two. That says something.

Part of the project required my team to gather and analyse intelligence on all OMGs in Queensland, and also to monitor any other OMGs trying to move into the state. Wingclipping gave me a new lease of life: not only was I travelling for surveillance operations, but I was now travelling to interstate BCIs and monitoring bikie events.

The Hells Angels had planned to have their 1993 World Run in South Australia. The public reason given for sending senior club members from every chapter in the world to meet in one place was to get together and party, but criminal intelligence received from Canadian and US law enforcement made it clear the more important reason was to meet and discuss business, including international drug distribution. While the Hells Angels and other OMGs admit there is criminal activity by some individuals in the clubs, they strenuously deny the clubs are criminal enterprises. But new alliances among the OMGs are formed and then abandoned pretty frequently and these changes were often marked by bombings, shootings and bashings.

Our brief from the ABCI was simple: we were to devise a strategy to disrupt the World Run based on evidence and criminal intelligence. What that meant for me was that I would be travelling around Australia over a couple of years working with BCI team leaders from all states and territories. This was my type of police work, working at a national level on a major project. By now I was a detective sergeant and I wanted to do this job for as long as possible.

One common problem faced by any criminal organisation is how to launder illegally obtained cash. Our intelligence indicated one of the more effective ways was through music festivals run by OMGs. If you had a truckload of cash, it was easy to sell tickets to a music festival and tell the tax office you'd sold twice as many. No records, cash cleaned.

I'd been to Victoria a few times as part of Wingclipping, and already knew the national teams well. This time I flew to Melbourne just before a Hells Angels concert to be held on a property a short drive from the country town of Broadford. Together with Wingclipping team leaders from the other states, we all met at the old Russell Street police headquarters in Melbourne. The locals gave us a briefing and, as was customary, we went out for a beer or ten to get to know each other. John, one of the Victoria BCI guys, was first shout.

As the barman poured the beers, John took out a fifty dollar note and held it in his hand, waiting to pay. 'Seen these around, Banksy?' he asked. The note had been stamped with the words HELLS ANGELS DRUG MONEY.

'I had a stamp made especially,' he said. 'I take out cash every payday and stamp every fifty with this. I reckon one day a few notes will turn up in the Hells Angels clubhouse and they'll think the Feds have marked all their cash. I fucking hate the Hells Angels.'

The following day we drove to Broadford. As they did for every Hells Angels concert, Victoria Police had set up a full roadblock on the dirt road about a kilometre or so from the entrance to the concert staffed by uniformed police, detectives from the stolen car and drug squads and us. Everyone going into the concert was stopped, breath-tested at the random breath-test booze bus and had their personal details recorded. Vehicles were checked for drugs, stolen property and guns. This was an excellent way of gathering information and intelligence. Local police also made several arrests. My job was to identify Queensland attendees and establish if any were members of Queensland OMGs. This would indicate alliances with the Hells Angels that we may not have been aware of.

Mid-morning on the first day, I was standing on the side of the road minding my own business taking photos of people and vehicles as they stopped at the roadblock. A drug squad detective I'd met briefly that morning strolled over.

'Hey mate, you're from Queensland, aren't you?' he asked.

'Sure am.'

'Well, I reckon you're in.'

'Sorry?' I lowered my camera.

Out of the corner of my eye I saw a tall brunette in black jeans and a T-shirt jogging over to where we stood. She stopped in front of us.

'Ignore what he said,' she said. I looked into her sparkling green eyes. 'All I said was you've got the best arse I've ever seen.' She smiled and I was smitten.

I looked back at her. She was still smiling. I forgot about taking photos of bikies.

I'd come to terms with the fact that my marriage was over, and that it was completely my fault. I hadn't formed any new relationships and didn't want to, but sometimes life presents other plans.

Jennifer had been in the Job for a few years and was a detective senior constable in the Drug Squad. She was a street cop like me but, unlike me, the Job hadn't jaded her. That meeting was the start of a long-distance relationship.

Unlike a lot of those relationships, ours worked. We travelled to see each other whenever we could, and I found myself imagining life with her well into the future. I thought about resigning and joining Victoria Police, but in those days I would have had to start as a junior constable again. Jennifer resolved things by resigning from the job she loved to move to Brisbane to be with me and started working in the hospitality industry.

I was happier than I'd been for a long time, but I was still haunted by the memories of the morning Pete was murdered and I still had the same bad dreams. Worse still, I was often trapped in my sleep by paralysis, hearing what was happening around me but unable to move. On other nights I'd have nightmares that were all about dread, and I'd wake in a cold sweat. I had told Jennifer about what had happened in detail and I knew she understood, but all she could do was comfort me when the dreams shook me awake.

But I did feel the sadness lifting and I was in love again. I wince at the thought of how my life might have gone if I hadn't been standing at that roadblock.

———

The World Run was disrupted and ultimately cancelled. The federal attorney-general had been fully briefed and, as a result of the evidence we'd gathered over two years, visa applications by many international Hells Angels were refused. No members, no meeting.

By 1993 I'd been in the BCI for three years and was starting to think about the next promotional opportunity. I still hadn't made my mind up when I bumped into a detective inspector I knew at police headquarters. He told me I needed 'to come back to the branch and into the fold' if I wanted to be promoted.

I respected him, listened to his advice and applied for a transfer to the Crime Operations Task Force. In mid-1993, I was placed into the Major Crime Squad, investigating mostly organised crime groups, instances of major fraud, extortion and large drug networks. Part of my job as a detective sergeant was to run covert operations involving undercover operatives. This gave me a chance to not only be involved in the covert world I loved, but more importantly it gave me the opportunity to look after the welfare of undercover operatives in a way Larry, I and the other undercovers hadn't been provided.

Once again it was off to the hairdresser and a clothing store, this time to smarten up.

ONE SUNNY DAY IN BRISBANE

Saturday 27 November 1993 was a beautiful day in Brisbane. I'd been in the Major Crime Squad for a while and was running two undercover operations. One of my undercover operatives had been on a buy that morning and I met him at a safe house to update the running sheet and other paperwork. I was dressed down, just in jeans and a polo shirt. I didn't look like a conventional detective sergeant by any stretch of the imagination. I liked it that way and took every opportunity to at least take off my tie, much to the chagrin of some bosses.

The night before, I'd been at the Police Club with my colleague Mick so, typically for a Saturday, we were both a little hungover. We felt a bit more human after a fast-food lunch and decided to head back to headquarters in Makerston Street via the city, where we could look at the attractive women strolling through town.

We were due to finish at 4 pm but ten minutes before 3 pm, as we were driving our covert car along Coronation Drive from Toowong, the unmistakable VKR tone signalling an urgent job sounded from the police radio under the dash. Mick and I stopped talking.

'Any unit in the vicinity of the MLC building, shots fired by a male in the foyer.' The VKR operator repeated this broadcast twice and we could hear units responding from around the CBD and suburbs.

I looked at Mick. 'We're not far, hold on.'

I activated the single tone siren and floored it. I thought of the worst-case scenario—of people being shot down by a gunman stalking through the building. The Hoddle Street and Queen Street massacres in Melbourne were in recent memory.

I had been issued with a five-shot Smith and Wesson revolver with a three-inch barrel. I regularly attended range training and was also a part-time Operational Survival Tactics instructor, so I was confident with the weapon. I carried it in a bum bag and told Mick to grab it from the back seat. We drove at high speed along Coronation Drive, weaving in and out of traffic, onto the Elizabeth Street exit and left onto George Street. I stopped the car about ten metres from the entrance to the MLC building and quickly scanned the area for signs of a gunman.

A Channel Nine camera operator was standing on the footpath directly in front of the entrance, aiming her camera inside. A few uniformed police were on the footpath as well and one was on the front steps of the MLC building. There was no cordon, and it didn't appear as if anyone was in charge.

I pulled my revolver out of the bag and stuffed two six-round speed strips into my front pocket. I was already in tactical mode, envisaging where I would stop and engage the offender if he left the building carrying a weapon.

I ran towards the camera operator.

'Police! Move away from there now!' I yelled.

Someone had to take control of the situation and quickly. In emergency situations people tend to wait to be told what to do, and this is true of some police as well. I don't say that unfairly, but at that time most police didn't have the training I did.

I instructed nearby officers to form an inner cordon and to call for a negotiator and the Special Emergency Response Team (SERT), the next evolution of the TRG, now totally full time. The presence of media and the public also needed to be restricted.

I ran up the stairs to the foyer and saw Mal, a uniformed sergeant, peering from behind a column. His firearm was still in his holster. I stopped beside him, using the column as cover. I didn't know if there were hostages in the building or not. The police communications operator had broadcast that the building had been cleared, but she was only broadcasting the information she'd been given. Never assume.

'Where is this prick?' I asked, a little louder than I should have. I still didn't know what to expect.

'He's in there, Banksy.' Mal jerked his head to indicate the foyer.

I still had my gun in my right hand when I heard a deep male voice say, 'Put your gun down or I'll blow this place up.'

I looked around the column and, as my vision adjusted, I made out an overweight bearded man with long dank hair sitting on the floor with his back against the rear wall. His legs were stretched in front of him and a rifle was cradled across his lap. I could see he had something in a box and what looked like old army webbing in front of the box.

The gunman and I were about four metres apart and looking at one another squarely in the eye. I had my gun at my side. *Okay,* I thought. *If he raises that rifle, I can take him from here; two or three to the chest and one or two to the head.* That was how I'd been trained. I was back in tactical mode. Any compassion I'd had was long gone.

I stepped further inside, towards where the gunman sat. I kept my gun at my side, pointed downward but ready if I needed it. The ceiling to the floor glass partition on my right had at least three bullet holes in it, but it was still intact. There were bullet casings on the floor. Sunlight streamed in through the main glass doors, but deeper inside the foyer was still shadowed. My hangover was gone and my old friend, adrenaline, was coursing through my body.

Cautiously I made my way forwards, keeping my eyes trained on the gunman's box. I wanted to see what he had in it. There were sticks of gelignite, and a lot of them. I tried to keep the fear off my face. He was also holding electrical wires and had a twelve-volt battery on the floor beside him. This was an improvised explosive device (IED). This situation had suddenly become a lot more serious.

I'd seen trained negotiators deal with high-risk offenders many times before, both in real life and in exercises. I raised my left hand slowly, palm outwards, in what I hoped was a calming gesture and said, 'It's okay, mate. I'm a police officer, just take it easy. I'll give my gun to this guy, okay?' I handed my gun to Mal, who was close behind me. I had sworn I'd never surrender my gun under any circumstance, but that box was full of enough gelignite sticks to kill the three of us and potentially whoever was outside. Mal still had his gun so, if it all went to shit, it would be up to him.

The gunman looked at me and then at Mal. 'Yeah, okay,' he said. 'Just don't do nothing quick. Turn around and show me your back. Then lift up your jeans, I don't want no ankle holsters.'

I turned to show him I was unarmed. 'Yep, no problem,' I said, trying to calm him. 'I'm not carrying anything else, mate. I'm not trying to trick you.' I lifted the left and right legs of my jeans to show him I had nothing there.

'Now I'll just show you my badge, okay? Just so you know I'm a copper.'

'Yeah, I want to make sure who you fucking are,' he growled.

I was standing there with a gun in my hand with half of Brisbane's police force behind me, so exactly who did he think I was? Maybe the bosses were right. Perhaps I should have worn a tie more often, even got a haircut.

I slowly removed my leather badge holder from my back pocket and opened it to show him, the sunlight gleaming off the badge.

He seemed satisfied. 'Yeah, okay, come in.'

Mal and I slowly moved further into the foyer. We were about two metres from him when he looked at me and said, 'Why don't you come in and have a talk. I won't hurt you.'

'No offence, mate,' I said with my hands raised to chest level, 'but I'm pretty scared and I don't want to get too close.'

I remembered that the first thing the negotiators I'd worked with did was to introduce themselves. 'Take it easy, mate. My name's Keith. What's yours?'

'Frank.'

'Is there anyone you want to see Frank?'

'Maybe a doctor. I've got no one. I'm alone,' he replied. He told me the name of a doctor he'd been seeing. I asked Mal to go outside and have someone call the doctor.

I took a good look at Frank. He was in his early forties and had shoulder-length black hair and a long black beard. He was dressed in jeans, old runners and a faded T-shirt. He was overweight and looked broken. He was smoking a cigarette with his left hand, which let him keep his right hand on the rifle. His finger lay across the trigger guard, exactly as taught in the military. It was then that I put two and two together and hoped I was wrong.

'What have you got in the box, Frank?' I asked.

He put his cigarette in his mouth and reached into the cardboard box. I thought he was going to detonate it there and then. Instead, he removed something and tossed it in my direction. I caught it with both hands. A third of a stick of gelignite. Bad enough on its own, but it was sweating, too. I hadn't been in the bomb squad for a few years, but I knew what that meant.

The substance leaking through the wrapping was nitro-glycerine, which meant the explosive was old and unstable. It could explode if knocked or dropped on the floor. My heart didn't just skip a beat; it skipped twenty.

Mal was now back in the foyer behind me. Even though I didn't know him, he was prepared to step into danger with me. I passed him the explosive.

'Mate, take this outside, and treat it very carefully,' I said.

I turned back to Frank to see he was grinning at me. 'You look like you could use a smoke,' he said. 'Want one?'

'Well, I gave up, but this probably isn't a bad time to start again,' I replied.

Frank slid a pack of cigarettes and a lighter across the floor to me. Smoking over unstable gelignite was not the smartest move, but there I was, sitting on the floor of the MLC building, facing someone with military training and armed with a rifle and a home-made bomb. I lit a cigarette.

'Thanks, Frank. So, what's going on, mate?'

'I'm fucken serious. These cunts have stolen from me and treated me like shit. I'm going to blow the whole place up and me too. I've got fifteen more sticks here and three dets wired up.'

Mal was back inside. He sat down close to the entrance. If it looked like Frank was about to do something stupid, Mal had given himself the chance to be up and gone. I couldn't blame him. I, on the other hand, would be royally screwed. There was no way I'd make it out before the bomb went off.

Frank's IED was straightforward. I could see three electric detonators and the detonator wires bared to expose the ends. All he had
to do was touch the ends to the positive and negative terminals on
the battery and there'd be bits of both of us raining across the river,
onto people strolling along Southbank enjoying their ice creams.

I considered diving over him to shove the battery out of the way
but discounted the idea. Even though I only topped out at eighty-
two kilograms, my weight falling on the box risked detonating the
unstable gelignite.

I looked down and noticed Frank's T-shirt. It had the Indian
motorcycle logo on it.

'You ride?' I asked.

'No,' he said. 'Just liked the shirt.' He looked over my shoulder
at the activity outside. 'If anybody comes through that door, I'm
blowing it. There's a cunt out there with a shotgun, get him away or
I'll fucking do it now.' He'd gone from calm to angry in a few seconds.

I tried to quieten him down. 'No one will come in, Frank. Can
you just let me go outside and I'll get them all to move back, okay?'

'Yeah, tell them all to fuck off.'

His agitation was scaring me. All it would take was a second
to touch the wires to the battery and it would all be dust and dark.

I walked to the door and yelled at the police outside to move
back. I couldn't see any bosses on the scene, but I knew they'd be
on the way.

'Okay, Frank, can I come back in?' I asked, turning back.

'Come in, just don't do nothing stupid. If you're fucken setting
me up, I'll blow us both.'

I walked back and sat down in front of him. I decided on a
straightforward approach. 'What would it take for you to hand me
the rifle? You don't need it to blow this place up.'

To my surprise, he looked at me and said, 'Yeah, I'll give it to you. But you need to get me a six pack, and I'm low on smokes.'

'Mate, a six pack is out of the question.' I paused. 'But I can probably get you a pot of beer. Let me see what I can do.'

Frank looked at me steadily, removed the magazine from the rifle and tossed it to me.

'That proves I'm fair dinkum, but I've still got one up the spout.'

'Thanks, Frank, I'll be back.' I stood up and walked outside.

The police presence had grown since Mal and I had gone inside, and there was now a team of SERT officers in single file pressed against the wall outside the entrance, fully kitted with vests, helmets and automatic weapons. Police cars lined the streets, and the media cameras were now all on the far corner of George and Adelaide streets. Plain-clothes officers wearing vests with 'POLICE' stencilled across the front, some of them brandishing shotguns, had formed an inner cordon. But more importantly there was now a commissioned officer on the scene, someone I knew would listen to me. Stoll had been with me on Operation Flashdance and had been recently promoted. He was on the Adelaide Street side of the entrance, right behind the SERT team, and was clearly ready to give the order to go once he'd received permission from the assistant commissioner. I walked up to him.

'Mate, I can get him out, I'm sure of it,' I said. 'But he's on edge, and we don't need to set him off.' I had a sense that Frank was in deeper than he intended and there was a chance I could get him out without loss of life: his, mine or anyone else's.

Stoll and I talked quickly and efficiently, the way we'd been trained. I described where the gunman was, his weapon, the IED and the risk factors. Then I hit him with my unusual request, the pot of beer.

'Well,' he said. 'We'll both get in the shit, but let's go with it.' Alcohol was strictly forbidden in a siege or hostage situation, but I didn't particularly care about rules that prevented resolution.

'If it goes bad, I'll be blown to pieces anyway and you can tell them it was all my fault,' I said.

Stoll broke into a grin. 'Deal.'

The young police around us, who didn't know our background, must have wondered why the boss in his pressed uniform with its shiny insignia was listening to this casually dressed, long-haired bloke.

A detective I knew well offered to get the cigarettes and beer. I asked Mal to bring them in when they arrived and went back inside to my new acquaintance.

'Frank, it's Keith. I'm alone and Mal is behind me,' I announced clearly at the front door. I walked inside and could hear my rational voice asking what the hell I was doing. Several things happen when you are very scared. Your senses kick into high alert, you see minute details with clarity and time seems to slow. I could see the beads of sweat on Frank's forehead and hear my heart beating. The glass partition beside us was starting to groan, its structure weakened by the bullets.

Mal walked in carrying the pot of beer. It looked damn good. He handed it to me with the cigarettes, and again eased himself onto the floor near the entrance. He was aware of the danger but continued to back me up.

I walked up to Frank and looked him in the eye. 'You first,' I said. I forced a smile and put the beer and cigarettes on the floor.

He handed me the rifle with his left hand, keeping his right with the bared wires near the battery. 'Just pull the lever down and forward.'

I pointed the rifle towards the wall and ejected the round. It fell to the floor and I picked it up. It had been fired.

'It was empty anyway, but thanks for the beer,' Frank chuckled.

'Mate, you've got me in the shit because I broke the rules for an empty weapon. Good one,' I said, bursting into genuine laughter and handing him the beer. I put the cigarettes on the floor closer to him. He took a long sip of the beer.

'I was getting sick of holding the bloody thing anyway.' He quickly gulped down the rest of the beer and lit another cigarette.

I started talking to him and asked what he'd done in his life for work. He'd worked in a lot of jobs but nothing serious after he'd 'come back'.

I knew it. 'Come back from where?' I asked.

'Vietnam.'

That's when I really started to worry. A lot of veterans I'd met were screwed up; quite a few were suicidal. He'd been a combat engineer, which explained why his IED looked so professional.

I'd finally found the common ground. I knew quite a few veterans, I said, and I'd spent a lot of time at Enoggera Army barracks on Anzac Day, Long Tan Day and Remembrance Day. If he understood our common ground, I was hopeful I could encourage him to walk out of the building with me. But then two things happened.

The first was the ding of an approaching lift. We both looked over as the doors opened to see a man in a business shirt and trousers stroll out. He was carrying a briefcase and walked with the aloofness of someone who has little time for the common folk.

I was pissed off because VKR had assured us that the building was locked down, but Frank went ballistic. 'Who the fuck is this,' he roared. 'You told me no one was coming in! Is he a fucking copper? Are you setting me up, you bastard?'

I was just as surprised as Frank. 'Take it easy, mate,' I said. 'I've got no idea who he is.' I got to my feet and turned to face the man. 'Who are you?'

Frank was more direct. 'Get the fuck away from me or I'll blow us all up, you cunt.'

The interloper looked shocked, but he managed to reply. 'I'll have you know I am a barrister and I happen to have an office on the fifteenth floor. I'm adjusting the air conditioning and you two are trespassing.'

'And I'm a police officer,' I said. 'I need you to get the fuck out of here before you cause any more trouble.'

Frank was screaming at him to get away. I don't know whether it was nervousness or arrogance, but the barrister looked down at Frank. 'If you don't leave, I'll be forced to call the police and have you removed,' he scoffed.

'I AM the police, you fucking idiot,' I told him as I grabbed his arm. 'And if you don't leave, I'm going to have you arrested. Now come with me and get out.'

I walked him forcefully to the entrance. 'Now fuck off, and don't come back in,' I yelled as I pushed him out and turned back to face Frank. 'It's okay, Frank,' I said, 'I didn't know he was here.'

Then I heard a footfall behind me and turned to see the barrister with a pen and notepad, following me back towards Frank.

'You have no right to talk to me like this,' he said. 'You are a very rude young man and if you really are a police officer I demand your name, rank and number, and you are obliged to provide them to me.'

'I'll be back in a minute,' I said to Frank, and turned to the barrister, this time grabbing him by the front of his crisp, ironed shirt. 'If you don't fuck off,' I growled, 'I am going to tear your head off. If you want my name, ask the four hundred police officers outside. Now come with me, you fucking clown, and this time stay out.'

I walked him all the way outside, shoved him towards the steps and yelled for someone to come and get this idiot out of here. The last I saw of my new friend was him being bundled out of sight by three police officers.

'Ah, Banksy, another happy member of the public,' Mal chuckled to himself.

I tried to gather myself and focus on the situation in front of me. I hoped that my little piece of street theatre had shown Frank that I was on his side.

But then, just as I was about to ask Frank if he was okay, the glass partition beside us finally yielded to the damage caused by the three bullets, shattered and crashed to the floor. Both of us jumped in fright. I'm sure Frank thought police were smashing their way in—they weren't—but there was a real danger that the force of the collapse would trigger the unstable gelignite. I braced myself for my trip to the other side.

For a few seconds after the ear-splitting smash of the glass we were silent. Frank looked at me. He was panicked. It was then that I realised he didn't really want to die. He lit yet another cigarette and I waited a moment to let the situation calm. I asked him again what had brought him here, and bit by bit he told me his story.

———

Frank quit the Army after he came back from Vietnam and, like many veterans, wandered from job to job. He'd met a woman and had a child. They separated, and he'd been paying child support when he could afford it. He knew he couldn't meet his obligations after losing another job, so he decided two days before I met him to make an appointment to talk to someone from MLC about cashing in his superannuation.

'I walked into the office and sat opposite this little smart arse in a tie who fucking laughed at me,' he said. 'He told me I was stupid to cash in anything because I'd have to pay fees and end up with nothing. They stole my money, all of it.'

The following day, during an evening drinking session at his favourite soccer club, he gave his dog tags to the barmaid.

The next morning he dug up the gelignite and the detonators he had buried in his backyard at Indooroopilly and constructed the IED. He put on his old army-issue webbing, loaded his rifle and slung it over his back. With the IED balanced in a cardboard box on the fuel tank of his trail bike, he rode into the city, a journey of about ten kilometres.

He parked the bike on the footpath in front of the MLC building, walked into the foyer and fired three shots through the glass partition. He told the security guard to leave and then sat down on the floor where I'd first seen him. He didn't want to hurt anybody. He just wanted to blow up the building and cause pain to the company. But in truth he had nothing to live for.

I'd had no plan to work through and just made it up as I went along. Now that the rifle was gone, I thought all I had to do was change his mind and persuade him to walk away from the bomb. But his mood kept swinging: one moment we'd be chuckling together and the next he'd be threatening to kill all three of us.

At one stage he looked at me sadly. 'Sorry, mate, I'm so fucked up I don't know what I think anymore.' I understood how the poor bastard felt.

I was confident we were making progress. All I had to do was get him to put the detonator wires down. But then he looked at me and said, 'Oh, I forgot to tell you I had this.' He reached into one of the webbing pockets and pulled out a hand grenade.

My first thought was: is this ever going to stop?

'I know what that is, Frank. Is it live?'

'It's live and I'm not fucken giving it up,' he said. 'I've had enough now. I'm going to do it, so you'd better go.' He put down the detonator wires and pulled out the grenade pin.

I'd never used a hand grenade, but knew that if he released the lever he was holding down I'd have five to seven seconds to get away. Once the grenade exploded, the gelignite would sympathetically explode and all three of us would be killed. It was highly probable that secondary shrapnel would be propelled in all directions, given the glass frontage of the building, killing or severely injuring dozens of police and reporters outside. I knew all of this, but my immediate response was anger.

'I've got enough nightmares in my life right now, Frank,' I lashed out at him. 'I'm not going to let you be another one. If you're going to do it, then do it. But I'm not leaving you by yourself.' I was damned if I was going to let this happen without a fight.

He looked at me for what seemed like an hour but was probably only seconds. 'You really aren't going, are you?'

'No, mate, I'm not. Now you're really fucking scaring me. Please put the pin back in, mate; if you drop that we're all gone.'

Out of the corner of my eye I could see Mal rising on his haunches, ready to spring out the door. I desperately wanted to do the same. My hands were shaking, and cold sweat was running down my back.

Frank didn't say a word. He slid the pin back into the grenade and handed it to me. I gave it to Mal, who took it outside. He was back quickly.

All I had to do now was persuade Frank to leave the IED. I thanked him for handing over the grenade and started to talk about how I could get him to his doctor if he walked out with me.

And then my pager gave an audible beep. Frank and I both jumped.

He glared at me. 'Tell the bastards you're busy with me.' It was clear that it was now Frank and me against everyone else. I might be able to win this.

I slowly took the pager from my belt, not wanting to set him off again. 'Hi honey,' it read. 'Where are you? You're late.' I laughed.

'What is it? What's going on?' Frank asked.

'It's my girlfriend. I was supposed to pick her up an hour ago. I'm in trouble.'

'Nah, it's alright. When you go home tonight and you tell her why, she'll understand.'

When you go home. I knew I had him.

I kept talking. The publicity would hurt MLC more than he realised, I said; he could have his revenge without hurting anyone or himself. I told him I'd stay with him and make sure he was treated well. I gave him my word that he wouldn't be handcuffed. Finally, he put the detonator wires on the floor away from the battery, and pushed the cardboard box forwards so he could stand up.

An hour and a half after I first entered that foyer, Frank and I walked out together. I placed him into an unmarked police car and sat beside him in the rear seat as we drove to the Royal Brisbane Hospital to have him admitted for psychiatric testing. There were no handcuffs.

I stayed with him. After a two-hour examination, the attending doctor told me he would not admit Frank to the psychiatric ward.

He rebuffed my observations about Frank's state of mind and said there was no evidence that he was suffering any form of mental condition. The waiting detectives took Frank away to be interviewed and charged with a string of offences.

I walked out to the unmarked car my mate Clarky had driven to the hospital and sat in the passenger seat. I breathed in deeply and let the stress seep out of my body. I suddenly felt very, very tired.

Clarky took me to headquarters. I rang Jennifer. Frank was right, she forgave me in a second. I then provided investigators with a long statement about the incident. It was signed and witnessed, and I was provided with a copy. Nearly an hour after we arrived, Clarky and I finally left headquarters and went across the road to the Police Club, where Jennifer was waiting with a group of my friends. Not one of them let me pay for a drink.

The next day's front pages were covered with photos of Frank, Mal and me. It was surreal to see photos of me plastered with the word 'hero'. I didn't feel like one at all, but I knew part of the old Keith had finally come back. I'd responded to the call with the intention of shooting a gunman, and instead I'd stopped him from killing himself. I felt like I had turned a corner.

When I reported to work at the Major Crime Squad office the following Monday, I was berated by a detective inspector for not wearing a tie on the weekend and not looking like a detective. Blah blah blah. I simply looked at him, turned away and walked into the squad office to standing applause from my mates. He didn't matter, they did.

Three days later I received a letter from the barrister I'd evicted from the building. It read in part: 'Once I left the MLC building after our interaction, I saw all the police outside and I was told what was happening. It disturbed me greatly and I had to go home and lie down. I now understand why you were using that type of language and I won't be taking any action.'

I gave evidence at Frank's committal hearing in the Magistrate's Court some months later. I looked over to the dock where he was sitting. I hadn't seen him since he'd been taken away from the hospital to be interviewed. He'd lost some weight, his hair was shorter and his beard trimmed. He looked back at me and nodded a greeting.

I walked past him after I left the witness box. He put out his hand to me and I stopped. His grip was firm as we shook hands and he looked me in the eye. 'Thanks for saving my life, mate,' he said.

I nodded back. 'Good luck, Frank,' I replied. I meant it.

Frank pleaded guilty and was sentenced to six years. Because of the publicity, his superannuation contributions were refunded by MLC without penalty. That made me smile.

Even all these years later, I sometimes think about Frank. I hope he found some peace.

A DIFFERENT WORLD

A few months after the MLC siege, I was moved to the Corrective Services Investigation Unit (CSIU) as part of the normal rotation of detectives in Crime Operations. Responsible for investigating offences ranging from the assaults and murders that occurred in every prison to deaths in custody and corruption by prison officers, the CSIU was funded by Corrective Services and staffed by police. It was one of the busiest offices I've ever worked in.

By the time I was transferred to the CSIU, Larry had returned from Europe and was a senior prison officer. The only way he could do anything in law enforcement was to join the Corrective Services department. He'd started as a junior prison officer and it was his goal to be appointed to the department's intelligence division. We sometimes ran into each other when I visited the prisons he was working in. He'd found his mojo again and had the sparkle in his eye that I had seen when I first met him all those years ago walking the beat.

But prisons are tough places to be. They have their own hierarchy and the weak are preyed on mercilessly. Assaults are commonplace; rapes almost as much so. There are regular stabbings with crude shivs made from sharpened toothbrushes or fashioned out of metal in the prison workshop. Prisoners are bashed with weights from the prison gym, often during gym sessions. A favourite way to inflict injury is to mix large quantities of jam or sugar in containers full of boiling water. The mix is thrown at the victim's face, with the sugar sticking to the skin to maximise damage. There are also better drugs inside prison than outside, smuggled in anally or vaginally by friends and partners. Even for a seasoned cop like me, this was a whole new world.

Every time I went into a prison to do a job, I would shudder when I heard those metal gates slam shut behind me. I was told of a prisoner who was suspected of informing to prison officers. A group of inmates lured him into the prison workshop during the change of shift when the officers were thin on the ground. They bashed him and bent him over a workbench. They removed his tracksuit pants and forced a narrow piece of PVC piping into his anus. Another inmate then fed a strand of barbed wire through the pipe to the end and pulled the pipe out, leaving the barbed wire inside the prisoner's intestine.

———

In mid-1994, a group of inmates started a fire in a wing of the Rockhampton Correctional Centre. I travelled to Rockhampton with one of the detectives in my team to investigate. When we arrived, the prison was still in lockdown with every inmate confined to his cell.

We started our interviews with the full list of inmates and their criminal history in front of us. A prisoner would be brought into the interview room, we'd introduce ourselves and start the questions. Some would be happy to tell us they had no comment, others would angrily tell us to get fucked but sometimes someone would actually talk to us because they saw a chance to improve their situation. (As CSIU detectives, we could have them transferred to a better prison or have them appointed to better jobs in the system.)

As we worked through the list, I saw a familiar name and laughed.

My colleague looked over at me. 'Okay, what's so funny?'

'I've just seen someone I know, but I haven't seen him for a long time. Just follow my lead on this,' I said.

My hair was much greyer than the last time I'd seen Michael John Parsons, but then so was his. I'd arrested him for assault in 1979 when I'd first worked at Mobiles. Years later, I'd been doing an undercover job in Brisbane when Parsons walked into the dealer's house. A heroin user, he shot up while I was waiting for my drug deal to finish. He also offered to sell me a few Buddha sticks. I saw him in the interview room after the operation was over and he'd been arrested. The last thing he said to me then was, 'I fucking knew I knew you.'

This was going to be fun. I kept my eyes down and pretended to read his history when the prison officer brought him in. We went through the usual introductions. He didn't react when he heard my name.

'Mr Parsons, you've got some interesting form,' I said. 'I see you were charged with assaulting police in 1979. What happened?'

'No big deal,' he said. 'Had a go at a copper after he pinched me.'

'And drug supply a few years later?' I asked.

'Yeah, I sold some sticks to a narc. Why are you asking?'

I looked up at him. 'Guess what? I'm back!'

He took a few seconds to register. 'Fuck me,' he laughed. 'How are you, mate? Not going to pretend you don't know me this time then?'

I realised then that there were benefits to my undercover life. I could talk to Parsons like a human being and not judge him for what he had done. And unlike a lot of my peers, I had empathy despite the darkness that still lurked beneath the surface.

Parsons and I had grown up on opposite sides of the fence, but we chatted like old mates. I sensed that he'd regretted his life and the actions that had brought him to prison time after time. I asked if he was using, and he proudly told me he'd kicked the habit. You can catch more flies with honey than vinegar.

'Okay, mate,' I said. 'What can you tell us about the fire?'

He shook his head. 'Sorry, can't help you. I'm not a dog. Bad things happen to people who talk to cops.'

'Yeah, I know that, but you have my word no one will know. All I need is for you to point me in the right direction. Nothing official. I can help you too.'

Parsons looked at me squarely. 'I want to go back to Brisbane,' he said.

I maintained eye contact. 'You help us, and your transfer is guaranteed.'

The silence in the room was waiting to be filled. 'Fuck it, I don't owe these cunts anything. Give me the list. If I was you, I'd talk to them,' he said pointing to some names.

I was a man of my word. Parsons was transferred to Brisbane's main prison soon after. I didn't cultivate him as a regular informant; I knew he wouldn't go for that and it's something I respected. But I also knew he was aware of the favour I'd done and that was part of the game. A few months later he was in the wing of a Brisbane prison when an inmate was murdered. He thought the way it had been done was cowardly, as a lot of prison murders are. When I spoke with him as part of the investigation, he suggested I look at two inmates. I'm sure he rationalised it in his own way, but the reality was he had become an informant. I like to think that he tried to do the right thing. Even if I'm wrong, I hold on to that thought.

———

It was then that I learned about what had happened to Harry. I'd lost contact with him, but knew that after he had been paid out by Queensland Police he'd turned to armed robbery to feed his heroin addiction. He left Brisbane on the run in 1993 and travelled to Adelaide on his Harley-Davidson. He committed more armed robberies there and was soon arrested. He'd used a a revolver but the robberies weren't violent. The judge found that his addiction had been a result of his undercover work and took this into account when sentencing him to three years in Yatala Prison.

Harry was later extradited to Brisbane, where he was sentenced to a further seven years. Even though it was acknowledged his undercover work had caused his addiction, his sentence wasn't reduced.

It still angers me that the Queensland Police never officially acknowledged how undercover work had damaged Harry's life; he was just quietly paid out and shown the door. I don't for one moment downplay the fact that he became an armed robber, but this was a direct result of volunteering for what he thought was a noble cause. The police who kept supplying him with heroin because it suited them to have an undercover cop who was a heroin user will never face the consequences.

SEVEN YEARS ON

I opened the letter from the Commissioner's Office addressed to Detective Sergeant K J Banks, CSIU, wondering what I'd done this time.

The Queensland Police Valour Award is the highest medal for bravery that can be awarded to a police officer in the state. The letter advised me that I'd been awarded this medal twice, one for the MLC siege and the other for Operation Flashdance. Peter Kidd would also be a recipient of a posthumous Valour Award. I still remember the surprise followed by the sadness that hit me.

I had always found it strange that recipients of medals tended not to speak about them, but now I understood why. While it was personally satisfying to be recognised for what we'd done, I didn't tell anyone in the office because I didn't want to seem boastful. It made me uneasy, but I know now that no one ever thought that. I rang Jennifer and she was thrilled; she knew what it meant.

A couple of days later, I was asked to attend the office of the Deputy Commissioner in company with Steve, Stoll and Geoff, who had all been on Operation Flashdance, as well as Mal, who had been with me at the MLC siege. We were congratulated individually before the deputy commissioner turned to me. 'Keith,' he said, 'Queensland Police history will be made on 29 July this year.

It will be the only time, I'm sure, that the Commissioner will be presenting two Valour Awards on the same day to a member of the Queensland Police Service.'

Then it hit me: 29 July. Seven years to the day since we'd lost Peter. To the day.

'Thank you, sir,' I replied quietly.

'There was a representation made by the District Court judge who sentenced the bomber from the MLC building to recommend you for an Australian government medal,' the deputy continued, 'but we don't double-dip in Queensland. I'd advise you to accept the Valour Awards because you never know what will happen in Canberra.'

I didn't give it any further thought. 'I'm very happy to accept a Queensland award, boss,' I shrugged.

A year later that same deputy commissioner handed me a letter from the Honours and Awards Secretariat in Canberra advising me that the Queen had approved the awarding of the Bravery Medal to Mal and me for our actions in the MLC siege. A member of the public had seen the media coverage and decided she would nominate us. Apparently she didn't think double-dipping was a problem. Since then, a policy has been introduced allowing police officers to be nominated for both state and federal awards.

On 29 July 1994, I was at the Oxley Police Academy to receive my Valour Awards. I was decorated by Commissioner Jim O'Sullivan along with other police in front of a graduating parade and hundreds of onlookers. Some of Jennifer's friends flew from Melbourne for the ceremony and stayed to celebrate. Interviewed by the media, I put on a brave face. I had been incredibly sad to see Peter's parents standing beside us to receive his Valour Award.

It took me fifteen years to put the citations for my medals on the wall. In the end it was Jennifer who persuaded me to do it.

THE PROBLEM IS . . .

Jennifer had been in the Job in Melbourne for almost ten years. She'd carried a gun, put on bullet-resistant vests and gone through her share of doors on raids. She'd also known a lot of members of Victoria's Special Operations Group and joked that all of them had the screw in their brains turned just a little too tightly. I had to agree with her; we *are* different.

We'd talk about the things we'd done and seen, like only cops can, and she understood, but death, suicide, violence and inhumanity didn't seem to affect her like they did me. She still had the sparkling green eyes and the effervescence that I had seen when I first met her.

Before she resigned and moved to Brisbane, I flew to Melbourne for her work Christmas party. All cops are parochial and I knew her workmates at Carlton CIB would be watching me like hawks, but I was surprised when Mark Wylie, who I'd met through Venny in 1988, leapt up from his seat in the restaurant and gave me a hug and a punch in the ribs. That, I came to learn, was his trademark sign of affection. Not long after I reconnected with him, Mark resigned from Victoria Police to accept a senior executive role with Myer Grace Bros. He travelled to Brisbane often and would always take me out to dinner, where we'd talk about the Master of Business degree he'd started.

On the surface he loved his new life. He was funny, engaging and great company but I could see he was still badly affected by his shooting in the house raid in 1986. Sometime during the second bottle of red wine he would talk about what happened and how he should have done things differently. I knew exactly what he meant. I looked forward to his visits and soaked up everything he said, but I always saw the sadness.

———

In late 1994 Jennifer and I began talking about our future. I'd been a detective sergeant for over four years and thought I should be applying for promotion, which meant going off the street and sitting behind a desk. At the same time, the Job I loved was destroying me emotionally. I was still looking for that rush of going through doors, as we often did when searching for prison escapees, but I knew my drinking to relax was happening more and more. I was still training, running and going to the gym, but that was so I could drink without consequence, in theory at least.

I had serious anxiety but never spoke about it. It was a feeling of dread in the pit of my stomach that never went away. My eyelid twitched relentlessly but I put that down to normal stress. Even though I still carried the list of symptoms I'd found in the library years before, I didn't realise how affected I was by what I'd seen and what I'd experienced as a police officer.

Jennifer and I discussed the idea of moving to Melbourne. She could have rejoined Victoria Police at her rank, but I would have been required to start as a junior constable. Instead, I applied for promotion to a detective senior sergeant position in Brisbane and was shortlisted for an interview. The nights before the interview were spent preparing for technical questions about legislation, procedure and so on. My conversations with Mark about management and organisational behaviour had taught me much more than my police experience, so I felt that I was a good candidate. I also had leadership and management experience and a police background that were unique compared to the other candidates.

One of the reforms of the Fitzgerald Inquiry was to introduce merit-based promotion but it hadn't been planned for nor had the consequences been considered. The result was an increased level of cronyism and favour seeking. If you had a senior officer as an unofficial sponsor, phone calls could be made to the panel convenor and your application treated very favourably. I know because I'd had a couple of calls suggesting I apply for particular promotions. I'd declined because I wanted to stay on the street, naively believing that my commitment to the Job would be rewarded later.

I saw many police promoted beyond their ability in the decade after the Inquiry, often from non-operational backgrounds with very little street experience. They performed well in interviews, had tertiary qualifications and, probably more importantly, had never been the subject of complaints from offenders. This suited the new age.

Despite what I thought about my candidacy for promotion, I wasn't successful. That was okay, I reasoned, I just needed to understand where I could improve. I asked for an appointment with the panel convenor, a superintendent, who told me I hadn't scored highly in emergency management and operational experience. I began to smell a rat.

I challenged his feedback, keeping my anger and disappointment under control, reminding him of the situations I'd been involved in and my experience in leading tactical, intelligence and investigative teams. After about forty minutes, the truth emerged at last.

'Okay. You want to know, I'll tell you,' the superintendent said. 'You need to change your personality.' He held up his hands, counting on each finger as he made his points.

'You're too outspoken. You challenge authority. You're too friendly with your troops. You need to be on our side of the fence, not theirs. And all the publicity doesn't help you either.' He sat back in his chair and steepled his fingers. I remember looking at him and feeling white heat coursing through my veins.

I don't yell when I'm angry, my voice drops. I spoke quietly and deliberately. 'With all due respect, sir [which is code for fuck you], I don't wake up in the morning, have a shower and shave and think to myself, *I'm going to find a siege today*. I just do my job. I'm outspoken and challenge authority, but only when people in authority make stupid fucking decisions that put my people or me at risk. As far as being friendly with my troops, we're a team and I'll always be like that with the men and women I go through doors with. That, sir, is what leadership is about. Finally, I don't seek publicity; it was out of my control. Your comments say it all: I don't need to take up any more of your day. Please be careful in here—you might get a nasty papercut. Thanks for your time.'

That was when I knew I didn't fit the mould, and probably never had. The Job had created who I was and now it didn't want me. I was too different. I realised with a jolt that Queensland Police post-Fitzgerald was more concerned with developing a corporate hologram than with protecting the public from predators. And that broke my heart.

About a week later, I had dinner with Mark when he was on another of his business trips to Brisbane. He asked if I was interested in a role in his Brisbane team that had become vacant. If I accepted, it was likely I would be promoted to a position in Melbourne within twelve months. His offer took me by surprise. I'd only ever been a cop, and I lived and breathed it. But I now knew that if I stayed a cop I'd have to sacrifice my style and personality and, like a bad marriage, I would come to resent it.

Mark and I had much in common. Like me, he came from a challenging background and spent his childhood in the tough housing commission flats in Flemington. He and his brother had grown up without a father and essentially had to fend for themselves. Their mother was at home, but a succession of men came and went.

I have never accepted the premise that criminals should be given a lighter sentence because of their challenging or deprived childhoods. Growing up in an environment of domestic abuse, with an absent father or with little money, is no excuse for a life of violent crime. Mark and I are examples of men who dragged ourselves up by our own bootstraps and chased our dreams of a better life. We are not the only ones. I've met many men and women who had difficult childhoods and made their way in the world without stealing or hurting others.

Given his upbringing and his friends, some of whom became notorious criminals in Melbourne, Mark could have easily gone down the path of crime, but he chose to join the police to do something worthwhile. He'd left the force for a better life and now he was offering me the chance to do the same.

'Why me?' I asked. 'Surely there are a lot of people you know who could do the job. I'm a cop, mate, and I don't know how to do anything else.'

Mark had a way of reading people. 'I like the way you challenge ideas and authority, and how you genuinely support people.' He picked up his glass of red. 'Besides, you've got two Valour Awards—that means you're not afraid to make decisions.'

This decision didn't take as long as I thought it would. I went home and sat down with a sheet of paper and divided it into two columns. At the top of one column I wrote 'Reasons to Go' and the other 'Reasons to Stay'.

Under the Reasons to Stay, I could only come up with:

- Camaraderie
- Job security
- Adrenaline.

I wrote down over twenty Reasons to Go.

I resigned a few weeks later. A couple of days after the paperwork was processed, I was summoned to the office of the Deputy Commissioner. I thought he was going to ask me to reconsider leaving, but he didn't know about my resignation. He wanted to formally congratulate me—Mal and I had been awarded the Australian Bravery Medal for our actions during the MLC building siege. He handed me the letter from the Federal Honours and Awards secretariat.

TRANSITION

It was Zulu's turn. He stood at the front of the room. Everyone was quiet. 'You should have seen him in uniform,' he said. 'One night I was in Queen Street and there's people everywhere. I was in plain clothes with my offsider sitting writing the log when this Mobiles car pulls up and out climbs the prettiest policeman I'd ever seen. Perfect ironed uniform, boots polished, hair just right, gun belt perfect. He puts his cap on just right and then strolls over to deal with some shit. That was the night I first met Banksy and we've been brothers ever since.'

Send offs are poignant, particularly when you're the one being sent off. As each person spoke, I was filled with mixed feelings. Had I made a mistake? Would I survive outside the Job? But I also knew my time was up. I couldn't stay in a job that was destroying me.

Zulu finished his speech by informing the room he'd made a bet that I'd be back in six months. I was born to be a copper, he said, and he knew I'd miss it too much.

He lost the bet.

—

Larry McGregor had been promoted to the Corrective Services Intelligence Unit around the time I started a new life outside the police. It was a transition for both of us, long removed from the days of undercover, living in the identities we assumed and losing our own in the process. He and I were the lucky ones: we came through it relatively okay. Larry had found his niche and I was leaving mine.

Harry was in prison in Brisbane and Spider would also fall prey to the addictions he'd formed when undercover. He'd been smoking pot every day since he came back from Mt Isa, and when he didn't have any pot he drank large amounts of booze. All this while he was working as a detective on the Gold Coast. In 1999, he was arrested for attempting to procure four hundred dollars from a man he was investigating for an assault; he'd offered to go easy on the charge in exchange for the money. The man was an informant for the Criminal Justice Commission and the conversations had been recorded.

For that stupid mistake, Spider was sentenced to four years imprisonment. In a lucky break, Larry was able to influence the system to get him to a prison farm; a general prison is not a healthy place for cops. One of the other prison farm inmates was an armed robber Spider had once extradited and driven to the Coast from Sydney. They'd stopped on the way and Spider bought him a couple of beers. In return for that kindness, this crook told the others to leave Spider alone.

By the time I resigned, I'd lost contact with Harry and Spider. Irish was gone and Desperate had transferred to the country to save his career. The only ones from the old undercover circle I still spoke to were Larry, Zulu and Steve and, even then, Larry was the only one I spoke to regularly.

—

About fifteen months after I resigned, Mark made good on his promise and we were living in Melbourne. It was like coming home.

I flew into Tullamarine Airport about six weeks before Jennifer and our baby daughter Karly followed. It seemed like it had rained for weeks without a break, but I didn't care. This was a new beginning, and I felt a lightness that I hadn't had for what seemed a lifetime.

The days of sharing basic motel rooms and saving travelling allowances were well and truly gone. This was a new world travelling from state to state and staying in fabulous hotel rooms by myself. Mark laughed on our first business trip when I asked if he and I would be sharing a room. 'We're executives, mate, we have our own rooms.'

Not only did Mark mentor me through the transition from policing to the corporate world, he also pushed me into pursuing tertiary education. He had experienced the benefits of study and he wanted to see me do the same. I enrolled in a Master of Business Administration. After the first semester I was hooked, graduating four years later.

Life went on and I was promoted progressively to more senior roles over the next few years with salary rises, increased benefits and travel. Anyone looking in from the outside would have thought I had the world at my feet. I had a great job, was building a network of friends across the country and could visit Brisbane often. We had another daughter, Julia, and had bought a lovely house in the leafy suburb of Lower Templestowe.

The reality was far different. The dread I had lived with since Peter's murder soon found me, and it stayed. I carried the sadness every day. If I was travelling alone, I'd often find myself thinking about Flashdance with a drink in my hand. When I was home,

I was short-tempered and agitated by small things. I never yelled at anyone, but I knew I carried anger just beneath the surface. I didn't know how to get better, and I didn't consider seeing a counsellor; I thought they were only for extreme cases.

Then one day in 2001 my phone rang. It was my youngest sister, who was still living in Charters Towers. 'Do you know someone called Spider?' she asked nervously.

Spider may have lost his job, but he was still an investigator. He'd remembered my sister's name and that's how he found me.

A few months later I landed in Coffs Harbour on the north coast of New South Wales. Spider met me at the airport and the years melted away. We were both older and still close mates, notwithstanding the years apart. We were bonded by the experience of undercover that few understand.

We spent the next three days catching up on the paths our lives had taken. Spider was obviously suffering and was on medication for anxiety and what I assumed were issues stemming from the past.

'Four hundred dollars, mate, was the price of a bag of pot and I was addicted,' he said, explaining his arrest and conviction. 'Despite what they say, you can get addicted to pot. I needed it to function. Simple as that, mate. I fucked up so I could buy pot.'

I didn't judge him then and I don't judge him now. Like all of us, he'd volunteered for undercover work for noble reasons and had been irrevocably changed as a result. That world had its consequences for Spider, just as it did for Harry and the others. I saw only the old Spider—the funny, engaging bloke who had been a major part of my life years before. I was happy to be in his company.

I could see why he loved living where he was: the beach was close by and it was isolated enough that it was unlikely strangers would pass through.

'Mate, how many times do you lock the door at night?' he asked me a couple of days later.

I laughed. 'I'm weird, mate, I need to make sure it's locked five or six times.'

He just nodded and we lapsed into a comfortable silence.

'If you get into a car and put your work briefcase on the back seat, do you stop about a hundred metres down the road and check if it's still there?'

I looked at him. 'In fact, yes I do. Do you?'

'Yep. What about anger?'

I told him about my white-hot anger with people and my agitation at home with stupid little things, like being cross if the phone rang or the doorbell sounded.

He just nodded again. 'You might have PTSD mate. The sooner you see someone the better. It took me way too long.'

I didn't say anything, but surely his comment about PTSD was over the top. I didn't have that. I was just short-tempered, probably because that was who I am. I didn't need to see a shrink; I wasn't too bad. Yes, I drank a bit more than most and maybe I was sad a lot of the time, but surely not PTSD—that happened to people who'd been in really bad things.

———

Back in Melbourne life went on. By 2006 I'd left retail and was now general manager of an Australasian security company with an office in South Melbourne. One afternoon I decided to grab a coffee from the café next door and, as I left our building, I froze in my tracks. I couldn't move and felt as if the world had collapsed on me. I was gripped by a massive panic attack. I took a step sideways and leant against a wall, trying to control my breathing.

My heart was racing, and I was paralysed with fear when my mobile rang. Mark had called to say hello. He heard my voice and knew what was happening. He drove across the busy suburbs of inner Melbourne and calmed me down.

'You're seeing this person tonight, no arguments. I've already made the appointment,' he said, handing me a business card.

That night I was sitting in a counsellor's office crying. Mark set me on the path to seek help and, while I wasn't diagnosed with PTSD until years later, I know that if he hadn't been there for me that day I might not be here now.

Despite his empathy and concern for the struggles of others, Mark could not beat his own darkness. He took his life in 2014, another casualty of the Russell Street bombing. I was blessed to have known him and to have called him a mate. He is often in my thoughts.

LIGHTNESS

When the Queensland tactical unit Special Emergency Response Team (SERT) was created in 1992 with all members of the team as full-time operators, the dream had at long last become a reality. Today SERT is a professional, superbly equipped and highly trained team of physically fit and committed police officers.

In 2012, a dual commemoration was organised in Brisbane to mark twenty-five years since Peter Kidd's murder and twenty years since SERT was established. Steve contacted me and urged me to attend, but I was hesitant. I'd made some early progress with my issues, but I still carried the guilt and anguish twenty-five years later and I was worried that people would blame me for not having done enough during Flashdance. Jennifer persuaded me to go.

The function was held at a pub in Southbank, once the haunt of vagrants and prostitutes but now a trendy and favoured destination in a very changed Brisbane. As I walked in, I was greeted by old friends who were genuinely happy to see me. There was a sombre commemoration of Pete followed by a scrolling loop of photos and news footage of SERT operations over the years playing on a large screen. I was looking at the screen when a young man in his twenties introduced himself. I shook his hand and said, 'I'm Keith Banks, nice to meet you.'

In a moment I will never forget, he answered, grinning, '*You're Keith Banks?* I thought you'd be bigger. It's a pleasure to meet you, mate. Can I introduce you to some of the other operators?'

I don't know what I'd expected. Certainly not derision, but I hadn't expected to be embraced into the circle as quickly as I had. I knew the SERT operators studied Operation Flashdance as part of their training (in fact, it had become a case study for all Australian tactical teams and the SAS), but I still carried guilt and thought I'd be judged for not being strong enough to insist on gas and distraction grenades.

I relaxed more and more as the night progressed. At the end of the formal function, about half a dozen of the SERT team who were not on call and were therefore allowed to drink corralled me. One of them, a tall, well-built man in his late twenties nicknamed Slick, put his hand on my shoulder and announced they were taking me into the casino for a drink.

It was after midnight and I was standing among these tough young men when it came out, my deep sadness rising again from where I'd pushed it down. 'Boys, I'd just like to say I hope you don't hold Flashdance too much against me,' I said.

The conversation stopped and for a terrifying second I thought I'd overstepped the mark. The anguish gripped me, and that voice inside told me I should have stayed quiet.

Slick looked at me. 'What the fuck are you talking about, brother? You're one of our heroes. You did a fantastic job and there's nothing more you could have done,' he said, wrapping his arm around my shoulders. 'Mate, it's an honour to meet you.' Suddenly another drink was placed in my hand.

I woke the next morning thinking how glad I was that I'd made the trip. Something was different now. Then I realised what it was.

The guilt I'd carried had been lifted from my shoulders. I felt light for the first time in many years. *'What the fuck are you talking about, brother? You're one of our heroes. You did a fantastic job and there's nothing more you could have done.'*

I walked to a nearby café, bought a coffee and made my way into the Botanical Gardens, to the same spot where we'd so often parked our Mobiles police cars over thirty years earlier to watch the sun rise before we finished work.

As I looked at the brown water of the Brisbane River, I could hear the voices and laughter of the men and women who had been my comrades. Many of them are gone now, but I have never forgotten them and the family of blue that I am so proud to have been part of.

I was finally at peace.

EPILOGUE: CLOSURE

In January 2015, Larry Philip McGregor died. My brother by choice had been battling blood cancer for over two years, facing it with the calmness and optimism typical of the Larry we knew and loved. A lapsed Catholic, he had converted to Buddhism years before and had been the happiest I had ever seen him. He'd remarried and was studying for a post-graduate degree. Life is not fair and never will be.

Larry had suddenly been rushed to hospital soon after Christmas and we spoke almost every day. Two days after our most recent chat I received a call from a close friend, who urged me to get to Brisbane as quickly as I could. I caught a flight that afternoon.

Zulu and I spent a few hours beside Larry's hospital bed as he lay unconscious in a coma. We talked to him about the old days, laughing and shedding tears. When we knew the time was right, we said goodbye. I leaned a little more forward, holding Larry's hand. I told him it was okay for him to go. We took one last look at him as we left the room. He died that night.

Larry's wife had asked that I give his eulogy. The Buddhist service would not take place for another week, so I stayed in Brisbane. Over the following days I made it my mission to track down as many former undercovers as I could. They were easy to find, except one, but I eventually succeeded in finding that last phone number. When Harry answered and I told him who I was, he cried. He guaranteed he'd be in Brisbane to say farewell to Larry.

Spider, Giblet, Chuck, Charlie and I met at a pub for lunch on the day of the service. During one of our final phone calls, Larry had told me he didn't want black suits or sad clothing to be worn at his funeral. 'I know you'll look after it, KJ,' he told me. 'The gaudier the better.' The boys all turned up wearing Hawaiian shirts, looking like they'd walked off the set of *Magnum PI*.

We'd only been in the pub for a few minutes when the doors to the pub opened and Harry tentatively walked to our table. His trademark smile was back, as was his trademark greeting. 'Boys!' he said. The years melted away. Harry had reinvented himself and his past life in prison was not important to any of us. He'd survived and that's all that mattered.

It was my honour to give Larry's eulogy. I hope I did him proud. As I spoke about the Larry we knew and loved, it was hard to ignore the massive splash of colour provided by the gaudy shirts worn by a group of middle-aged men at the rear of the room. When I looked at them, I didn't see them as they were then. Instead, they'd been transformed into what they'd been all those years ago, young and full of life, not knowing or caring what the future held.

I still miss Larry every day, I miss his calm voice and support in times of trouble and his wicked sense of humour. But I am comforted by the fact that his death resulted in me reconnecting with my other brothers who I'd not seen for many years.

I have now been a civilian longer than I was a cop, but I will forever be a veteran. My PTSD was finally diagnosed in 2019 and that diagnosis has empowered me. I now know I wasn't imagining it. Once you know something is tangible, you can start to fix it.

My need to work in dangerous and exciting areas as a cop had a consequence but it has shaped who I am today, for good and bad. The past cannot be changed by dwelling there. It took me a long time to learn that lesson and I am thankful I finally did.

Being a Queensland cop had its challenges in the bad old days, but I will always be proud of my service. I had the honour and the pleasure to work beside the finest men and women I will ever know. The few who were corrupt should never be allowed to besmirch the reputation of the many, who literally put their lives on the line to protect the people of Queensland. Of those men and women, there were too many who paid the ultimate price. They will never be forgotten.

I'm learning to let the anger and the darkness go. It's taken a long time for me to understand how to do that, and I now find myself smiling at memories of those days and of those friends, both absent and present. The sadness that followed me for so many years has finally lifted.

Go easy, my brothers and sisters in blue, wherever you serve. This is for you.

ACKNOWLEDGEMENTS

Sound, sound the clarion, fill the fife!
Throughout the sensual world proclaim,
One crowded hour of glorious life
Is worth an age without a name.

Thomas Osbert Mordaunt from 'The Call', 1791

I owe an immense debt of gratitude to the many people who have helped me through the journey from my first clumsy chapters to becoming a published author. This is a new and exciting world for me, and one I never imagined I would inhabit. It has been an incredibly cathartic experience and has undoubtedly helped in my ongoing recovery from PTSD.

Firstly, to my beautiful wife Jennifer. You have been my rock over many challenging years and without your love and support, I would not be the person I am now and my story would not have been told. I have not been an easy person to live with and throughout the emotionally tough times caused by my PTSD, you have been the glue that has held our family together. I can never tell you enough how special you are. You and our daughters Karly and Julia have taught me what unconditional love means and you are making me a better man. I love you.

Thank you to Richard Walsh for reading the first chapters of this book and in your unique fashion giving me the words of encouragement I needed to hear. I would not have achieved this without your belief in me, your guidance, your humour and your continuing enthusiasm for my story. Thank you, my friend.

Kay Danes, you are a legend. I can never thank you enough for introducing my first work to Richard, your absolute selflessness in encouraging and supporting me, your words of advice and for just being a wonderful human being.

To Rebecca Kaiser and the team at Allen & Unwin, who are incredibly supportive, welcoming and totally professional, thank you. You and your team have once again been a pleasure to work with. Thank you for taking my frequent calls and always making me laugh.

To Ben Smith, my co-author of *Drugs, Guns and Lies*, thank you for your help with some early parts of what would become my second published work. I wish you well.

To all you RHTCs in the tactical world, I was proud to be one of you, and will always be one of you in my heart. You are the tip of the spear.

My Brother in Arms, Scot Warwick aka Slick. I will never be able to tell you enough how much your affirmation lifted me from the dark morass of guilt I lived with for years and how much you changed who I was. Go well brother, you are a good man.

My old friend, Scott Nicholson, police veteran and world traveller. Thank you for all your enthusiastic support and advice in marketing my first book and your continued help with my second. You have done all this for me with no expectation of reward and that is the mark of a true mate.

To everyone who loved my first book *Drugs Guns and Lies*, including many of you who I have never met, thank you for your support and particular thanks to those who contacted me with personal messages of support and positivity. That has been one of the many joys of this experience and it is incredibly humbling.

To my former police colleagues who allowed me to tell your stories. Wendy, Steve and Trevor, thank you for trusting me. I hope I've been successful in bringing your stories to life.

To those of you who lived through some of these experiences with me, thank you for standing beside me in those days and for helping me tell those stories accurately.

To Mary McGregor, thank you for allowing me access to Larry's undercover notebooks and ensuring I could do his memory justice, both in this book and in my previous one. He was a special human being and is sorely missed by many.

Finally, to my former colleagues and current cops everywhere, you have contributed to a better world. Thank you for your service.

AUTHOR'S NOTE—LOOKING FOR HELP

Writing so openly about my struggles with PTSD, depression and darkness has been challenging. To admit to the world at large that I am not the perfect human I strove to be and that I am somewhat broken by my experiences was harder than I ever imagined. But I count myself fortunate when compared to many others who have much more to contend with because of their journeys.

It is my fervent hope that if anyone who is struggling with their world reads my story, it will help them understand that they are *not* alone and that what they are feeling is not something they have exaggerated or imagined.

If this is you, there are several organisations you can reach out to without fear of judgement.

Beyond Blue and Lifeline are two that are well established and provide valuable help. However, there are other organisations that are as equally supportive but not as well known.

The words mental health no longer hold the stigma they once did. At last, the conversation has evolved from speaking about mental health in quiet corners and undertones to one of speaking openly and often.

Part of this change is understanding that post-traumatic stress is not a disorder but rather an injury. Victoria is leading this evolution among first responders with the formation of Police Veterans Victoria, working in conjunction with Victoria Police and the Victoria Police Association.

Police Veterans Victoria is a not-for-profit organisation providing support for Victoria Police veterans and their families, who may be experiencing a range of mental health issues such as PTSD, depression, anxiety, grief, social isolation, and alcohol and substance abuse. Veteran peer support officers, all of whom are police veterans, volunteer their time to provide confidential support, resources and referral services including to psychologists and clergy. The organisation's philosophy is the belief that individuals who have shared experiences of life issues can better relate to other people trying to deal with similar issues.

www.policeveteransvic.org.au or contact@policeveteransvic.org.au

Blue HOPE Queensland is a volunteer organisation that provides support to current and former police officers and their families. Its founders have designed and implemented a tangible, external and completely anonymous service to help deal with the many significant psychological challenges that accompany operational policing. Based in Brisbane's Eagle Farm, the Blue HOPE facility has its own psychologist, physical therapist and personal trainers completely dedicated to providing much needed support to the thin blue line.

www.facebook.com/HelpingOutPoliceEverywhere,
www.bluehope.org.au or 1300 002583

The Male Hug is a not-for-profit organisation that aims to raise awareness on the issue of men's mental health and to encourage men to talk in a safe and friendly space. It offers programs and support for men who need somebody to talk to through the Lets Chat Buddy programme which is available 24/7. The organisation was founded by Tony Rabah, a Melbourne accountant who saw a great need for a platform enabling and encouraging men to gather in a safe and friendly environment to talk openly without judgement on mental health issues. The Male Hug has a vision to remove the negative stigma associated with this vital issue.

www.themalehug.com.au

No matter who you are, or what your lived experience may be, you are not alone.